MW00897198

Basic ROBLOX Lua Programming

By: Brandon LaRouche

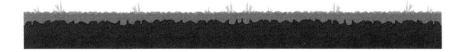

Chapter 0

Table of Contents

Chapter 1

Intro

This Chapter will go into detail about what you will need to begin programming in ROBLOX Lua. Included will be beginner instructions and a list of requirements. Also there will be a description on how this book will be set up.

Requirements

1. **A ROBLOX Account** - Free to register at ROBLOX.com

2. **ROBLOX Studio** - Downloadable at ROBLOX.com

3. **ROBLOX Game Client** - Downloadable at ROBLOX.com

ROBLOX is a free-to-play online building game. Anyone can register for free at ROBLOX.com.

Contained within this book is an intro to the basics of programming with ROBLOX Lua. ROBLOX Lua is a coding language created solely by ROBLOX for its users to create their online building games with. Behind ROBLOX Lua is the non-simplified Lua language, which is a light-weight computer language. A less important detail is that it can be translated from the Portuguese word "Lua" into the English word "Moon". The developers of ROBLOX have simplified Lua in ways that present easier functions and calls that are unique to the game of ROBLOX. Also, it makes the language much easier for younger kids to understand.

One of ROBLOX's main achievements is the introduction of coding to a young user base. Along with priding themselves on the entrepreneurship and business skills, is the increased interest among ROBLOX users to continue with their programming skills outside of ROBLOX.

As you read this book you will be faced with several tutorials, all of which will have fully accessible source-code that you can download via the Internet. You can find links to this code at the end of the book.

Info - Book Setup

Inside of this book are explanations to the basics of Lua Programming. This book will certainly not turn you into ROBLOX's best game creator over-night but it will start you on your journey to a successful ROBLOX experience.

As you progress through this book you will face a pattern in the content of each chapter. Most often you will complete a tutorial and then have a chapter of explanations related to either the chapter you had just finished, or the upcoming chapter.

Along with these tutorials are the full source codes, which will be listed near the end of the book.

Once you start progressing through the book, the difficulty level of the Tutorials will increase, along with the script size.

By the end of this book you should be familiar with the ROBLOX Studio. You should also be able to complete basic scripts with the knowledge of the format.

Chapter 2

Basics of ROBLOX Lua

Within this chapter you will read about the basics of ROBLOX Lua that will allow you to begin programming in ROBLOX. After this chapter you will also be able to navigate around ROBLOX studio to simply create and edit a script.

This chapter will cover all of the basics of ROBLOX and will grant you the ground knowledge for some of the key terms used throughout the book. If you have already had prior experiences with ROBLOX programming you still may want to consider reading this chapter, I recommend not to just skip over it.

Setup as the container of the ROBLOX Lua programming language a **script**. A script serves as a special text-file that contains a portion of your game's overall code. A game can have practically as few/many scripts as you want, and any script can be as simple or as complicated as needed. The act of coding a script in ROBLOX Lua is commonly referred to as scripting. Scripts are the only editable documents in a ROBLOX edit scenario that allow you to program code that works hand-in-hand with your game.

In a ROBLOX game the **Workspace** serves as an organizing container/folder for all of your game components. These components can be anything in the ROBLOX game. They have the same appearance to every user playing a game. Basically, everything you drag into the game and want active, such as a **brick**, should be located in the workspace. Scripts can be located here too! Another location for scripts to be located is the **Lighting** folder. This folder can contain every object that does not need to be seen in the actual ROBLOX game, as every object placed in this folder is initially hidden (invisible). You can also customize the time of day (brightness and sun/moon positioning), skybox (game background), by changing the Lightning folder's properties.

All objects in a game can be viewed in a side panel called the **Explorer Panel**. The Explorer panel is categorized by different folders including the Workspace and Lighting. You will also see the **Players** folder which contains all of the player's individual contents in a game, such as a **PlayerGui**; Which is a folder containing users active **GUI**(s). The word GUI stands for *graphical user interface*, in other words its an object in overlaying 2D layer on the user's screen (ex. leaderboard). Also you will see the **StarterGui,** which is where you put all of your created GUI(s) into for them to be added to a player's PlayerGui when they enter a game. There is also a **StarterPack** folder, which is where you place any gear that you want a player to receive when they spawn or respawn. Lastly, there are the **Debris** and **SoundService** folders, but this book will not go into much detail on them.

A **property** of an item is a manipulatable feature or quality of any object in a ROBLOX Game. Depending on the type of object, the properties that can be manipulated will change. Properties can be changed in the **Property Panel** in ROBLOX Studio while using Edit Mode. The Property Panel is a panel/sidebar displaying all properties found in an object. See *Figure 1* for a closer look at the Property Panel and Explorer Panel.

Throughout this whole book you will see the words **ROBLOX Studio**, which is ROBLOX's downloadable client that enables **Edit Mode** for advanced building in games. This is separate from the ROBLOX game client. Edit Mode is a mode in ROBLOX Studio that offers a more advanced building environment than the normal Build Mode. Included are many panels and an increased number of testing features such as redo/undo, rotate, pause-play-stop, etc. Programming is made easier in Edit Mode because it allows for the game's physics to be paused so you do not ruin your game.

With **Build Mode**, which is ROBLOX's classical building environment the game's physics are constantly running your avatar is always present to use in-game building tools. If your main goal on ROBLOX is to program with ROBLOX Lua you should always consider using Edit Mode for its pause and play features. You can do a live simulation of the script, then reset it. ROBLOX Studio is the only ROBLOX client that offers Edit Mode.

After reading this chapter you should have a basic understanding of the key ROBLOX Studio elements that you will see when you program on ROBLOX. On the next text page is a reference guide to all of the bold terms in this chapter.

14

Overview - Basic Components

1. **Script** - A special text-file that contains a portion of a game's overall code.

2. **Scripting** - The act of programming a script in ROBLOX Lua.

3. **Workspace** - Serves as an organizing container/folder for all of your game components.

4. **Brick** - The basic component of a ROBLOX game, it is a virtual brick that you build with.

5. **Lighting** - A folder that contains every object that does not need to be seen in the actual ROBLOX game.

6. **Explorer Panel** - A side panel showing all of the folders and groups of a game's content.

7. **Players (*Folder*)** - A folder, which contains all of the player's individual content in a game.

8. **PlayerGUI** - A folder containing users' active GUI(s).

9. **GUI** - Stands for *graphical user interface*; an object in an overlaying 2D layer on the user's screen (ex. leaderboard).

10. **StarterGui** - Where all user-created GUI(s) are placed into in order for it to be added to a player's PlayerGui when they enter a game.

11. **StarterPack -** Where any gear is placed that a player will receive when they spawn or respawn.

12. **Debris -** A folder in the Explorer Panel which is not discussed much in this book.

13. **SoundService -** A folder in the Explorer Panel which is not discussed much in this book.

14. **Property -** A manipulatable feature or quality of any object in a ROBLOX Game.

15. **Property Panel -** A panel displaying all properties of an object that can be changed.

16. **ROBLOX Studio -** ROBLOX's downloadable client that enables Edit Mode for advanced building in games. This is separate from the ROBLOX game client.

17. **Edit Mode -** A mode in ROBLOX Studio that offers a more advanced building environment than the normal Build Mode. Included are many panels and an increased number of features options such as redo/undo, rotate, pause-play-stop, etc. Programming is made easier in Edit Mode, which allows for the game's physics to be paused so other scripts or a objects do not ruin your game.

18. **Build Mode -** ROBLOX's classical building environment in which the game's physics are constantly running and user's avatar is present to use in-game building tools.

Chapter 3

Tutorial – 1 Setting Up A Game

This Chapter will go into detail about what you will need to begin programming in ROBLOX Lua. Included will be beginner instructions and a list of requirements. Also there will be a description of how this book will be set up.

On ROBLOX the first step to creating a successful game is to configure it with the best setting that fit your needs. This tutorial will start you on your way to prepare your own game.

First, you must go to your **Places** page in any web browser. Then, simply click "View Place" on the game you wish to configure. Once viewing the **Game's Page** go to the **Options** drop-down button, which is located to the right of your avatar's picture. In the drop-down select **Configure This Place**; this is where you can manipulate your game's settings. The layout the **Configure Place Page** is fairly similar to as it would appear on your game's page. Please note that you can change these settings at any given time and that you can only change the settings of your own game.

To begin, let's set your place's **Description** to something like "This is a really cool game!". When setting your place's description it is important to consider what your game is about. Everyone that goes to play your place can see the place description and will be influenced by what you include. Personally, I try to add only an important summary or tips on how to play, plus a link to a **VIP**

Shirt if I have one. VIP Shirts can be sold to a user for extra features in a game. Next, you can change your place's **Name** to something catchy like "Epic Game". This is the most important aspect of your place's settings. Try to keep the Name short and sweet because it's the first thing a player will look at on the **Games Page** to decide whether or not to play your game.

Once you scroll down the page you will see a box labeled **Place Type**, here you can set your game up as a **Game Place** or as a **Personal Server**. A Game Place is a game that only you can edit, but anyone can enter. The second choice, a Personal Server is a mode that other players can build in and have their changes automatically saved periodically. For details on these two types you can hover your mouse over the (?) buttons. In this tutorial I am going to choose a Game Place. It will not be a game that I need other players to build in.

After setting up the Place Type you will be able to set the **Player Limit** to mandate the amount of players allowed in your game at one time on an individual **Server**. Inside of this category there are two options, **Classic Place** - with a max of 20 players or a **Mega Place** with and set server size of 30 (may increase in a later update). Since I do not need a large server for this tutorial I am going to leave the setting on Classic Place.

This next feature is great for testing a game or spending some quality time with your friends without interruptions. As you may see, this feature is **Access/Privileges** and controls the privacy levels of a game. Included are two levels of privacy to choose from, either **Public** or **Friends Only**. If your game is meant to be a game that anyone can play, you should choose Public. However, if you want a game that restricts players that can play with you, choose Friends Only, which makes it so only players on your friends list can join you in a game. These settings apply to every server of a game, if you want a server Public or Friends only every new server created will follow the same rules. So, existing servers will remain unchanged.

Below the Access/Privileges box is a box labeled **Copy Protection**. Copy Protection only has one option, it can be turned on or off, and the option is called **Copy-Lock**. If Copy-Lock is on it locks your game so that no other user besides you can access the build or edit mode. On the other mode, if Copy-Lock is off, any player can access your game and all of its content through build or edit mode. Thankfully, even if Copy-Lock is off and users can access the content of your game, they still are not able to save changes; they can only save the game as a file to their computer. I am going to keep this tutorial's game with Copy-Lock disabled because I will be allowing you to download the full content of the game.

When you have chosen whether to Copy-Lock or not Copy-Lock your place, you can move on to the options labeled **Turn Comments On/Off**. The title gives away what the options do, you can either chose to allow commenting or not allow commenting on your game. Commenting is a feature on your game's page where anyone can leave a comment, this opens up for spam, false reviews, or useless posts. Please do keep in mind that you cannot manage comments posted, but you can turn comments on/off at any time. For all purposes of this tutorial it does not matter whether I have commenting enabled so I will leave it as it is as enabled.

When you are done changing your commenting options you will see that below is **Chat Settings**. Chat settings manage the in-game chat appearance by three choices. First, is **Classic Chat**, a chat that appears as an overlaying GUI in the upper left corner of the game window. Second is **Bubble Chat,** which creates a bubble with the user's typed message over their head. If you want to put a GUI in the upper left corner of the game, you may want to choose Bubble Chat. Lastly, there is the **Both Chats** option that grants the ability to use both types of chat in your game, Classic Chat and Bubble Chat. This tutorial will use the Both option.

Following the Chat Settings is the **Genre** setting. ROBLOX categorizes every game by the assigned genre that it is given. The choices will be listed below, but try to pick a category that best fits your game's theme. If you have no clue what genre your game should be, leave it as All, which is the default setting. Most of the categories are self-explanatory, but if you are confused just look at the icon next to the choice or go to the Games Page and see some of the games under each category. This tutorial will be under the Tutorial Genre. Here is a table of the choices:

Category	Description
All	Default - Every Genre
Town and City	Role-Playing Life Games
Fantasy	Magic Games (ex. RPG)
Sci-Fi	Space/Futuristic Games
Ninja	(ex. Samurai)
Scary	Horror Games
Pirate	Pirate/Ship Battle Games
Adventure	RPG/Exploration Games
Sports	(ex. Football)
Funny	Humorous Games (ex. Quiz)
Wild West	Cowboy/Western Games
War	(ex. World War I)
Skate Park	Only Skateboard Games
Tutorial	Games That Teach Players

One of the last options is **Gear Settings,** which can directly correspond with the game's Genre. There are two main options, you can allow All Genres of gear to be used in your game or Only Genres that match your game's genre. After these main options are more specific options to allow certain individual Gear Types into your game. Again I will include the choices in a table below. Gear can influence your place's gameplay greatly, so try to pick gear that will not hinder the game experience for any user. For example, you would want to allow Social Items into a Cafe game but not Explosives. Here is a table of the Choices:

Gear Category	Example
Melee Weapons	Sword
Ranged Weapons	Bow and Arrow
Explosives	Dynamite
Power Ups	Speed Potion
Navigation Enhancers	Compass
Musical Instruments	Guitar
Social Items	Sign
Building Tools	Paint Bucket
Personal Transport	Skateboard

Second to last is the **Reset Place** option where you can revert your game to a preset map. You can choose one of four choices. These choices are

Happy Home in Robloxia, Starting BrickBattle Map, Empty Baseplate, or Personal Server Starting Place. By default you game is a Happy Home in Robloxia, but if you want to create a new game from scratch you should reset to an Empty Baseplate. An Empty Baseplate comes with one large brick that acts as the ground that you can either delete or build on top of. I will reset back to an Empty Baseplate for this tutorial.

Last comes the **Version History** box where you can see a list of all previous times you have saved the game. If you would like to revert to a different version of your game, the list is in chronological order. To revert simply click the "[Make Current]" button next to the designated save. This tutorial has no past saves, so will will leave it alone.

Most importantly you must make sure you save your changes. All you have to do is click "Save Changes" right below the Version History. Once you have saved the Page will refresh and you can click the button labeled "Back" right next to the edit Name text-box. This will take you back to your game's main page. You can see any changes that you have made except for any in-game options such as Chat type. If you have reverted to an old save or reset to a preset map it may take a few minutes for the game's thumbnail picture to appear because it is going through a moderation process.

To review the key points of this chapter, you can read the **Overview** that follows.

Overview – Settings & Related

1. **Places -** The page of a user's account on ROBLOX showing a list of all of their games.

2. **Game's Page -** The webpage dedicated to an individual game on ROBLOX.

3. **Options -** A drop-down button which is located to the right of your a user's picture on one of their Game's Page.

4. **Configure This Place -** A button in the Options drop-down button.

5. **Configure Place Page -** Where a user can manipulate their game's settings.

6. **Description -** Description of a game seen by any user.

7. **VIP Shirt -** Clothing sold to a user for extra features in a game, most commonly sold as a t-shirt.

8. **Name -** Title or Name of a game seen by any user.

9. **Games Page -** One of the main pages on ROBLOX.com where you can see a list of user games.

10. **Place Type -** Where a game can be set up as a Game Place or as a Personal Server.

11. **Game Place -** A game that only the user who created the game can edit, but anyone can enter.

12. **Personal Server -** A mode that any player can build in and have their changes automatically saved.

13. **Player Limit -** The amount of players allowed into your game at one time on an individual Server.

14. **Server -** An individual instance of any game, an additional server is created whenever the Player Limit has been reached.

15. **Classic Place -** A game with a max Player Limit of 20 players on one server.

16. **Mega Place -** A game with a set Player Limit of 30 (may increase in a later update).

17. **Access/Privileges -** The privacy level of a game.

18. **Public -** A game that anyone can play.

19. **Friends Only -** A game where only players on the game creator's friends list can play.

20. **Copy Protection -** Controls access levels to a game's content towards other users.

21. **Copy-Lock -** If enabled, it locks a game so that no other user besides the game's creator can access the build or edit mode.

22. **Turn Comments On/Off -** Options that control if a game allows user commenting.

23. **Chat Settings -** Manage the the in-game chat appearance by three choices.

24. **Classic Chat -** A chat that appears as an overlaying GUI in the upper left corner of the game window on a user's screen

25. **Bubble Chat -** If enabled it creates a bubble with the user's typed message over their head when they chat.

26. **Both Chats -** Grants the ability to use both Classic Chat and Bubble Chat in a game.

27. **Genre -** A chosen category that matches a game's theme and is used in order for ROBLOX to be able to organize games.

28. **Gear Settings -** Options to allow All Genres of gear to be used in a game, Only Genres that match a game's genre, or Specific types of gear.

29. **Reset Place -** Where a game can be reverted to a preset map.

30. **Version History -** Where the game's creator can see a list of all previous times they have saved their game. This is also where a game can be reverted back to a previous save.

31. **Overview -** Section at the end of each Chapter of this book that defines key words.

Chapter 4

ROBLOX Studio Elements

In this chapter you will learn about the components of ROBLOX Studio that will assist you with your scripting.

In the world of ROBLOX Lua Programming your best friend is ROBLOX Studio. ROBLOX Studio serves as a ROBLOX **Game Engine**, where you do all of your scripting and building. There are various **Scripting Tools** and Panels that are initially hidden but can be opened up for an enhanced programming experience.

Most of these can be viewed by selecting them under the **View** pull-down of the **File Bar**. Here is a simple table. Following the table will be more detailed descriptions of every item.

View	Description
Toolbox	Object catalog and inventory
Explorer	Shows objects and components of game
Property	Shows properties of selected items
Output	Activity console for ROBLOX games
Diagnostics	Shows Performance of game and scripts
Task Scheduler	Displays game errors

In the table, the first item is the **Toolbox**. The Toolbox is a panel that serves as a **Catalog** for all ROBLOX items that can be added into a ROBLOX game. These are objects such as **Free Models**, **My Models**, **Decals**, **Packages**, and pre-made ROBLOX models. It is easy to add items from the Toolbox into your game; you can either double-click on them or drag them directly into the game. When inserting any object the Toolbox is the best place to look.

Second in the table is the Explorer. In the Explorer you can see a list off everything contained by your game. You can select different items in the Explorer to view their properties. The Explorer contains groupings that act as different folders for the game's items. *Chapter Two* summarizes all of these main groupings.

Next in the table is the Property Panel. This panel displays all of the properties belonging to the currently selected object in the Explorer. In the Property Panel you can manipulate certain properties of an item, or use the properties to be referenced in a script. For example, this is where you can change the Name of any object or the color or a Brick.

Fourth in the table is the **Output**. The Output serves as an activity console that shows you the events that ROBLOX Studio has processed. You can see events that only relate to the ROBLOX Studio such as plugins loading or errors. Also, you can see script errors. This console acts as the best way to find out why and where your script's code is breaking.

Fifth in the table is the game **Diagnostics**. A game's Diagnostics shows the performance of your running ROBLOX game. You can also see the performance of running scripts. It's an advanced version of the Output console.

Lastly comes the **Task Scheduler**. Displayed by the Task Scheduler are ROBLOX errors. You can see all of the current tasks being performed by ROBLOX Studio such as mesh rendering.

Following these explanations will now be some images of the components in action:

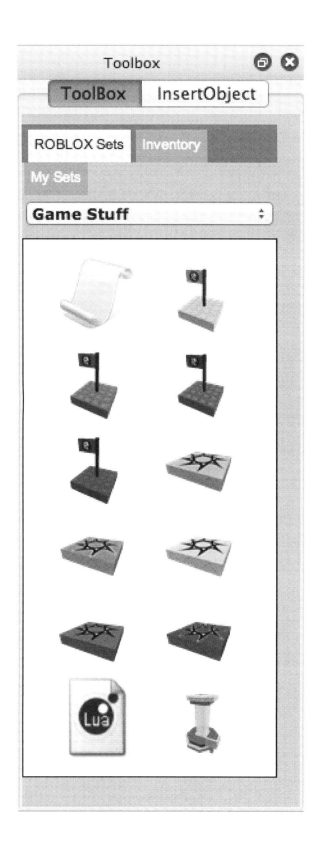

34

Property	

Part "Part"

Search Properties

Property	Value
Appearance	
BrickColor	☐ Medium …
Material	Plastic
Reflectance	0
Transparency	0
Data	
ClassName	Part
Name	Part
Parent	Workspace
▶ Position	0, 3.4, 0.5
▶ RotVelocity	0, 0, 0
▶ Velocity	0, 0, 0
Behavior	
Anchored	☐
Archivable	☑
CanCollide	☑
Locked	☐
ResizeIncre…	1
▶ ResizeableFa…	Right, Top, …

Output

Plateaus Plugin Loaded
Roads Plugin Loaded
Input Info Plugin Loaded
Wed Feb 8 20:11:39 2012 - CoreGui.RobloxGui.Resizer:14: attempt to index local 'controlFrame' (a nil value)
Wed Feb 8 20:11:39 2012 - Script "CoreGui.RobloxGui.Resizer", Line 14
Wed Feb 8 20:11:39 2012 - stack end
Wed Feb 8 20:11:39 2012 - **BuildTools is not a valid member of ScreenGui**
Wed Feb 8 20:11:39 2012 - Script "CoreGui.RobloxGui.SubMenuBuilder", Line 16
Wed Feb 8 20:11:39 2012 - stack end
Terrain Plugin Loaded
Elevation Plugin Loaded
Elevation Plugin Loaded
Craters Plugin Loaded
Orbs Plugin Loaded
Time of Day Plugin Loaded

Command >

Sleep: 13.7 Wait:

Task Scheduler

Name		Error	Priority	Activity	Rate	CV	Time
▼	Arbiter:Place5						
◉	Heartbeat	1.01	101.3	0.6%	29....	3.8%	0.000s
z^z	MeshCo...						
z^z	None M...						
z^z	Physics	1.01	101.3	0.0%	29....	3.8%	0.000s
z^z	PropGrid						
z^z	Read Ma...						
z^z	Render	0.51	3.4	15.1%	58....	13.4%	0.003s
z^z	RenderR...	0.51	51.2	0.2%	58....	2.0%	0.000s
z^z	Sound	1.01	101.1	0.0%	29....	3.8%	0.000s
z^z	Texture...						
z^z	UserInput	1.03	102.5	0.0%	58....	2.0%	0.000s
z^z	UserInp...						
z^z	Write Ma...						

Overview – ROBLOX Studio Elements

1. **Game Engine -** A program that assists in building games. They handle physics, compiling code, interface layout, and ease up on the workload and experience required to create games.

2. **Scripting Tools -** Tools that help you with your scripting in ROBLOX Studio.

3. **View (*Pull Down*) -** Contains the option to show or hide many helpful scripting tools.

4. **File Bar -** The top bar with different tabs such as *File* or *View*.

5. **Toolbox -** A panel, which serves as a Catalog for any ROBLOX item that can be added into a ROBLOX game.

6. **Catalog -** A collection of items. On ROBLOX it is a collection of all assets created by users and staff.

7. **Free Models -** Models shared by other users in the public domain that is free for anyone to use.

8. **My Models -** Models that can be found in a user's inventory.

9. **Decals -** Images uploaded to ROBLOX and

approved by the moderators.

10. **Packages -** Groupings of Free Models made by a user.

11. **Output -** An activity console that shows you the events that ROBLOX Studio has processed successfully or unsuccessfully.

12. **Diagnostic -** A panel that shows the performance of your running ROBLOX game.

13. **Task Scheduler -** A view that displays all of the current tasks being performed by ROBLOX Studio such as mesh rendering.

Chapter 5

Tutorial 2 – Hello World

In this chapter you will face your second tutorial comprised of the basic teachings on how to display a simple message saying "Hello World".

This is the second tutorial, in this tutorial you will learn how to display a simple message displaying the text "Hello World".

To begin let's setup a new place just like we did in *Chapter 3* as a new Empty Baseplate. Using ROBLOX Studio go into the place in Edit Mode. Next, add a script by clicking:

Insert -> Object -> Script

This is in the top File Bar. Once you have inserted a script double-click the script in your Explorer Panel to open it in a **Script Editor**. A script editor is a new window in ROBLOX Studio that acts as a color-coded text editor for ROBLOX scripts.

For any script that you plan to create it helps to define all of the objects you will be using with a **local** reference. With a definition you can access objects with a common name instead of a long reference string of code. Also, **local** references stay defined for the entire Script. If you do not use **local** the reference will only work inside the individual **function**. You can use a **local** reference with this format:

local reference = object

Now whenever you want to call **object** you can use reference.

Another helpful tool is commenting, to write a comment you just type "--" before you type the text. Here is an example:

-- Comment type here

Commenting can be useful if you are planning to share the script or edit it later. Also you can use comments to divide a script or knock out lines of code that you are not using but want to remember.

Now that you know those two helpful methods we can move on to the actual tutorial. This script short and only takes up five lines of code, also this code will only run once because it has no **function**s or repeats. We will start by defining a new **local** instance of a message to be displayed plus we will include a comment to describe the code. Type the following code:

local Message = Instance.new("Message") -- Defines a new instance of a message for the entire script

Seeing that we have our **local** definition of a new message we can call Message and setup some configurations. First, we need to set the text of the message. Use the following code below:

Message.text = "Hello World" -- Sets text of the message

When the message will be displayed, now it has something to display and will read "Hello World". Next, we should give the message a location in our **Workspace** - which always needs to be capitalized. The type of message we are displaying will appear right away as we add it into our game, so enter the code below:

Message.Parent = game.Workspace -- Our message is now   inside of the Workspace

Using the term .**Parent** means that it is Parented by our workspace, just like a chapter in a book. Lastly, lets add some addition code that will **wait**(5) meaning that it will wait five seconds then we want to :**Remove**() the message from our game. It's quite easy to do, just type the following:

wait(5) -- Waits 5 seconds

Message:Remove () -- Removes our message

That wraps up our script, so it will now add a message into the game's **Workspace** reading "Hello World" and the remove it after five seconds.

In the end, if you copied all of the code included in the tutorial, your code should look like this:

local Message = Instance.new("Message") -- Defines a new instance of a message for the entire script

Message.text = "Hello World" -- Sets text of the message

Message.Parent = game.Workspace -- Our message is now inside of the Workspace

wait(5) -- Waits 5 seconds

Message:Remove () -- Removes our message

Personally, I like to separate different sections of my code by skipping a line, this does not alter the way the code works, it just adds a little organization and is optional.

If your code matches up let's save our progress

by going back into the **Game Window** then exiting and saving. After you have successfully saved go back into the game with Edit Mode. Finally you are ready to test! In order to test, you must go into a **Play Solo** mode. Play solo is a test mode with a private server and a only one character; A private environment of your game. You can enter this mode by clicking the following in the top File Bar of ROBLOX Studio:

Tools -> Test -> Play Solo

Then a new window should open with a private environment of your game with a **Test Player** named "Player". If the script works, you will see the message appear and then disappear after five seconds, but if it does not work go back and double check you code. Now you can save and exit to complete the tutorial.

Overview – Hello World

1. **Script Editor -** A new window in ROBLOX Studio that acts as a color-coded text editor for ROBLOX scripts.

2. **local -** A definition that allows access to objects with a common name instead of a long reference string of code.

3. **Comment -** Text comments that mark your code but do not change the functionality of a script. A comment is marked by "--".

4. **Parent -** Term that means that an object is Parented by another object (ex. Workspace is Parented by the Game).

5. **Game Window -** A window in ROBLOX Studio that allows you to view and edit your game, visible in Edit Mode.

6. **Play Solo -** A test mode with a private server and only one character; A private environment of your game.

7. **Test Player -** A player in Edit Mode's Play Solo named "Player".

Chapter 6

Brick Properties

Before we move on to scripting anything that involves a Brick or Part, I will first briefly show you the basic properties that they contain.

Grouping	Property	Description
Appearance	BrickColor	Color of Brick
	Material	(ex. Wood, metal)
	Reflectance	Shininess/Luster
	Transparency	Translucency
Data	ClassName	Not changeable
	Name	Your name for object
	Parent	Object parented by
	Position	Physical location
	RotVelocity	Rotating X, Y, Z
	Velocity	Moving X, Y, Z
Behavior	Anchored	Ability to move
	Archivable	Ability to be cloned
	CanCollide	Solid or not
	Locked	Selectable or not
Behavior	ResizeIncrement	Not changeable
	ResizableFaces	Not changeable

Part	Elasticity	Flexibility
	FormFactor	(ex. Brick, plate)
	Friction	Slipperiness
	Shape	(ex. Ball, block)
	Size	Size of object - **Stud**
Surface Inputs	BackParamA	Number Value
	BackParamB	Number Value
	BackSurfaceInput	(ex, NoInput, steer)
	FrontParamA	Number Value
	FrontParamB	Number Value
	FrontSurfaceInput	(ex, NoInput, steer)
	LeftParamB	Number Value
Surface Inputs	LeftSurfaceInput	(ex, NoInput, steer)
	RightParamA	Number Value
	RightParamB	Number Value
	RightSurfaceInput	
	TopParamA	Number Value
	TopParamB	Number Value
	TopSurfaceInput	(ex, NoInput, steer)

Surface	BackSurface	**Surface Connection** type
	BottomSurface	**Surface Connection** type
	FrontSurface	**Surface Connection** type
	LeftSurface	**Surface Connection** type
	RightSurface	**Surface Connection** type
	TopSurface	**Surface Connection** type

As you can see, there are very many properties of a Brick or Part, and most of them are not used by a beginning scripter. All of these are viewable in the Property Panel only when you have a Brick or Part Selected.

Here are some brief summaries of the main categories:

All of the Properties in the **Appearance** grouping are visual. Any change made to this category can be seen in Edit Mode.

In the **Data** grouping are changes including the

traits of a Brick or Part, both physically unseen.

The **Behavior** grouping has to do with the way users can interact with a Part.

Included in the **Part** category controls a Brick's or Part's interaction with the environment. A Brick or Part has a size system based off of a measurement called a **Stud**.

I will skip the **Surface Inputs** grouping and head right to the **Surface** grouping. Within this grouping is the control over the **Surface Connection** of a Brick or Part. A Surface Connection is the type and strength of the hold between the sides of two objects.

Overview – Brick Properties

1. **Appearance** - Visual characteristic viewable in Edit Mode.

2. **Data** - Physical and unseen traits of a Brick or Part.

3. **Behavior** - Grouping that has to do with the way users can interact with a Brick or Part.

4. **Part (*Grouping*)** - Category controlling a Brick's or Part's interaction with the environment.

5. **Stud** - One unit of measurement for an object in a ROBLOX game.

6. **Surface Inputs** - *Not covered in this chapter.*

7. **Surface** - This grouping is the control over the Surface Connection of a Brick or Part.

8. **Surface Connection** - The type and strength of the hold between the sides of two objects.

Tutorial 3 – Color Changing Door

In this chapter you will learn how to create a door in ROBLOX that also changes color on touch.

Throughout this chapter you will work on completing the third tutorial in this book. During this tutorial you will learn how to script a Brick into a **Door** that changes color as you walk through it.

To start, we will begin with an Empty Baseplate and enter the game with ROBLOX Studio in Edit Mode. Now, add a **Part** by clicking this in the File Bar:

Insert -> Object -> Part

Once you have added a Part, click on it in the Explorer to select it. When you have selected the Part you can now add a script into it by choosing the following from the File Bar:

Insert -> Object -> Script

Great, now you are ready to start scripting. Double-click on the newly added script in the Explorer to open the Script Editor. Make sue you clear the script, and then you can continue with writing our own script.

First, we need to declare the door that we will be using as a **local** named **Door**. The first line of code in your script should look like this:

local Door = script.Parent -- Defines our new Door
as the Part's Parent

Remember, the term **script.Parent** refers to the object the the script is a subclass/child to, so in this case it is Parented by the Part we added earlier.

Unlike the last Tutorial, we will now be using a **function** so that the script only triggers when a certain action takes place. To start of a **function** we use this line of code:

function onTouch() -- Sets the start of our function

This is only the start of a **function**; an **end** closes off a **function**, which we will add in later.

The code that we will be using to make Door work will be between our **function** and the **end**. In this code we will first have to make the door open and then after waiting some time we will need it to close. Let's start by opening the door and making it semi-transparent with the following code:

Door.CanCollide = **false** -- Our door is no longer solid

Door.Transparency = 0.5 -- Our door is now partially

transparent

Before we continue, I will explain what we just coded. In a Brick or Part the property CanCollide determines if a Part is sold or not. This is determined by the two states of **true** meaning solid or **false** meaning that the Brick or Part is not Solid. In this step of the script we need to be able to walk through the door so we set CanCollide as **false**. After this we change the Transparency to 0.5, which is the halfway point between the minimum value of 0 and the maximum value of 1.

We want to add a special effect to this door so it will change **Color** when it opens. Yet, we can do even better than just changing the color to another specific color, we will make it change to a random color. Add the following to your script:

```
Door.BrickColor = BrickColor:Random() -- We have
   assigned a randomly generated color to our Door
```

Above we call upon the BrickColor property of our Door. Instead of setting the BrickColor to a set color, which works off of a number system (see: http://wiki.roblox.com/index.php/Colors), we use BrickColor:Random() to generate a random color.

Finally our door is set to open, but we also want it to close back up. In order to do this we will first have to add:

```
wait(2) -- Waits 2 seconds
```

We add a wait so that the door stays open for enough time to walk through before we close it. It's simple to close the door, so we can just do the reverse of everything we did to open the door. Your next few lines of code should look like this:

```
Door.CanCollide = true -- Our door is now
                completely solid

Door.Transparency = 0 -- Our door is now non-
                transparent

Door.BrickColor = BrickColor:Random() -- We have
assigned another randomly generated color to our
                Door
```

All of that code should top off our **function** that we can now call to a close with:

```
end
```

However we are not quite done yet, in order for

our **function** to work correctly we need to set it up to be triggered when our **Door** is **Touched**. This only takes one line of code that follows the **end** that we just declared. Write in the following code:

Door.Touched:connect(onTouch)

With that code we have connected our **Door** to our **function** onTouch() by using **connect** and naming it as **onTouch**.

Our script should be successfully completed, so now you should recheck that your code looks like the following:

local Door = script.Parent -- Defines our new Door as the Part's Parent

function onTouch() -- Sets the start of our function

Door.CanCollide = **false** -- Our door is no longer solid

Door.Transparency = 0.5 -- Our door is now partially transparent

Door.BrickColor = BrickColor:Random() -- We have assigned a randomly generated color to our Door

```
wait(2) -- Waits 2 seconds

Door.CanCollide = true -- Our door is now
                         completely solid

Door.Transparency = 0 -- Our door is now non-
                         transparent

Door.BrickColor = BrickColor:Random() -- We have
assigned another randomly generated color to our
                      Door

end

Door.Touched:connect(onTouch)
```

If your code matches up correctly with the code above, you should go back to the Game Window to save and exit your game. Then, re-enter your game in Edit Mode of ROBLOX Studio and enter Play Solo in the File Bar by doing the following:

Tools -> Test -> Play Solo

After opening Play Solo you can test your Door. If your door works correctly it should open for two seconds and change color then close and change color. Lastly, you can exit Play Solo and go back to your Game Window to save and exit. You have successfully completed this tutorial!

Overview – Color Changing Door

1. **Door** - A Brick or Part that opens and closes to allow a player to enter an area.

2. **Part** - Also known as a Brick. The basic component of a ROBLOX game, it is a virtual Part that you build with.

3. **function** - An action that restrict the script to only trigger when a certain action takes place.

4. **end** - A call that closes a **function**.

5. **CanCollide** - Property of a brick that determines if a brick is solid or not.

6. **true/false** - Two choices of certain properties that enable or disable the property.

7. **Transparency** - The level of translucence of an object.

8. **Color** - The color of an object.

9. **BrickColor** - The color of a Brick or Part that is based off of a number system.

10. **Random** - An unpredictably generated property.

11. **Touched** - Registers that an object was

touched by a humanoid.

Chapter 8

Tutorial 4 – VIP Door

In this chapter you will learn how to make a VIP door that only works when wearing the correct t-shirt.

This chapter is a slight sequel to the last chapter, and instead of a color changing door that anyone can walk through, you will learn how to make a VIP only door. The whole concept behind a **VIP Door** is that in order to get past, you must be wearing the correct item of clothing. VIP doors are commonly used for in-game bonuses because they require you to spend ROBLOX currency on the actual item. For most games, the money will come more from the **VIP Shirt** that from the place visits. Just a little side note, you make tickets per every visit to your game, but only one from a user per day.

With this tutorial you will make a VIP door that checks if the user is wearing the correct item, then decides to open or close. Once deciding to open or close, the door will either open for the particular user, or kill them.

We are going to start this tutorial just like most of the other tutorials, so you will need to go into an Empty Baseplate in Edit Mode of ROBLOX Studio. After you have entered Edit Mode you will need to add a part by doing the following in the File Bar (*I will tell you this in every tutorial*):

Insert -> Object -> Part

Now select the part that you have just added by clicking on it in the Explorer. Since you have selected the Part, you can add a new script directly into it. While remaining selected on the Part add a script by doing this in the File Bar:

Insert -> Object -> Script

Good, now let's resize the Part to look more like a door with the **Resize Tool**. This resize tool is located among the icons on the top bar of ROBLOX Studio.

Enter the Script Editor by double-clicking on the script we just added into our Part. Clear the script to prepare for adding our own code.

First, we need to declare our Door, so we will use a **local** named **Door**. For the first line of code in your new script, type:

local Door = script.Parent -- Declare the Part as Door

This **Door** will be the main object that all actions of our script work around.

To start of our **function**, will need to declare it before all of our events can take place. However since we will need to find out some information about the user that touches the brick, the t-shirt, we will make it special. I'll explain the code after, but for now just code in:

function onTouch(Brick) -- Sets the start of our function and when triggered it gives Brick, the object that was hit

The special addition in this **function**, is the Brick inside of its (). This reference to Brick allows us to find out what object touched our Door to trigger the **function**. In our case, we want to detect the user who touched our Door in order to check what t-shirt they are wearing.

However, there is a flaw in the code above. By the way of the **function** it will run even if another Part touches our Door. To counteract this we must check to make sure that the object that Brick refers contains a valid **Humanoid**. A Humanoid is a special component that can be added to an object to give it life properties in ROBLOX such as health. In order to do this we will try to find the Hominoid in a **local**, then check to see if it exists. So, let's use this code:

local Player =
Brick.Parent:findFirstChild("Humanoid") -- Finds Humanoid in Brick

When we used the term :findFirstChild("Humanoid") we were searching **Brick** for an item with the **ClassName** of Humanoid. With this **local** we can now verify that it exists and that **Brick** is a real user. To do this we will use an **if** and **then function**. Use the following code:

if (Player ~= **nil**) **then** -- Checks if Player is a real Player

An **if** check if Player ~= **nil**, which means that if Player is not equal to nothing **then** the script can continue. Just like a **function**, an **if** must have an **end**, and we will declare that later.

If all of the work we did to check if the user exists passes runs successfully, we will be able to now check if the user is wearing the correct VIP Shirt. Again we will use an **if** and **then function**. Since we can now use Player as an object's destination, we can edit its content. Incorporate the following line into your script:

if Player.Parent.Torso.roblox.Texture ==
"http://www.roblox.com/asset/?version=1&id=10285
94" then

You can find this location in **Player** we found. Inside of **Player** there is its **Torso** which contains a Decal named **roblox** to display the t-shirt that the user is wearing. Any Decal has a **Texture** contains a link of the image the Decal represents. We can compare this decal to the link of our desired t-shirt. You can find this link by replacing the number in the URL above with the numbers in your t-shirt's URL on ROBLOX, but subtract one. For this example my t-shirt had 1028595 in the link so I used 1028594.

Finally, if all of our tests have proven successful and there is a real user wearing our VIP Shirt we can make the door open. I am going to merge al of this code together because it is the same from *Tutorial 3* where we made color changing Door. Add the next few lines:

Door.CanCollide = **false** -- Our door is no longer
solid

Door.Transparency = 0.5 -- Our door is now partially transparent

Door.BrickColor = BrickColor:Random() -- We have assigned a randomly generated color to our Door

wait(2) -- Waits 2 seconds

Door.CanCollide = **true** -- Our door is now completely solid

Door.Transparency = 0 -- Our door is now non-transparent

Door.BrickColor = BrickColor:Random() -- We have assigned another randomly generated color to our Door

Once this code is triggered, the door will open, change colors, become semi-transparent, and then revert back to its original closed state with another random color.

We are now ready to do something when our **Player** is not wearing the VIP Shirt. To to this we will use an **else** function. Every **else** used only works after a corresponding **if** has been declared, because its an alternative. Not every **if** needs an

else, they are optional, but you can also have one and leave it empty. To call an **else** for our script, use this code:

else Player.Health = 0 -- Deny access and Kill the Character

Users contain a **Health** value in their Humanoid, which when set to 0 kills them. We take advantage of this easy process, and set the **Health** of **Player** to 0 to kill them when they are rejected by the door.

To end off all of the **function**s and **if**s we will need to add multiple **end**s. Since we need to figure out the correct number of **end**s we can count up what they correspond to. We will need one for our **function** and two for the two **if**s. That adds up to three ends in the end of our script. If we do not have the right amount, the script will not work, and you can see the error displayed in the Output. Add our three ends to close of our actions:

end

end

end

All of our actions are finally closed off, so we can connect our **function** to our Door being touched. This will be the last line in our script:

Door.Touched:connect(onTouch)

Your script is now complete and should look like this:

local Door = script.Parent -- Declare the Part as Door

function onTouch(Brick) -- Sets the start of our function and when triggered it gives Brick, the object that was hit

local Player = Brick.Parent:findFirstChild("Humanoid") -- Finds Humanoid in Brick

if (Player ~= **nil**) **then** -- Checks if Player is a real Player

if Player.Parent.Torso.roblox.Texture == "http://www.roblox.com/asset/?version=1&id=10285 94" **then**

Door.CanCollide = **false** -- Our door is no longer

```
                    solid

Door.Transparency = 0.5 -- Our door is now partially
                    transparent

Door.BrickColor = BrickColor:Random() -- We have
assigned a randomly generated color to our Door

            wait(2) -- Waits 2 seconds

Door.CanCollide = true -- Our door is now
            completely solid

Door.Transparency = 0 -- Our door is now non-
                    transparent

Door.BrickColor = BrickColor:Random() -- We have
assigned another randomly generated color to our
                    Door

else Player.Health = 0 -- Deny access and Kill the
                    Character

                    end

                    end

                    end

        Door.Touched:connect(onTouch)
```

Let's return to the Game Window so you can save and exit the game. After you have saved and exited your game, you can return to the game in Edit Mode of ROBLOX Studio. Then, you can go into the game in Play Solo to see if your Door works correctly. Even in Play Solo, your Test Player will wear any clothes as your real Character, so you may wear the VIP Shirt. If you do not remember how to go into Play Solo, just go into the File Bar like this:

Tools -> Test -> Play Solo

Okay, now that you are in the game, you should be able to test the door. If your are not wearing the VIP Shirt, it will kill you, but if you are wearing the VIP Shirt it should perform its open and close actions. You may now return to the Game Window. Lastly, if your test was not successful, just verify that you have copied down all of the correct code.

You're almost done with the tutorial, all you must do now is save and exit. You have now completed *Tutorial 4*.

However, if you want to do something extra you can build a **VIP Room** for **Door**. Add a few more

Parts and resize them to form a wall around the door, like a house. Inside of this VIP Room you can put anything that you want to restrict access to. For instance, you could fill the VIP Room with **Giver**s. A Giver is a Brick that inserts a **Tool** into the Player when they touch it. This additional step is not needed, but it would be good practice to make your door have a purpose.

Overview – VIP Door

1. **VIP Door** - Door that only opens for a user wearing a corresponding item of clothing.

2. **VIP Shirt** - Shirt that grants special abilities in a game.

3. **:findFirstChild**("") - Searches for a designated item's Classname in the identified object or grouping.

4. **Humanoid** - A special component that can be added to an object to give it life properties in ROBLOX such as health. Any Player contains a Humanoid.

5. **if** - Used to compare values in scripts to determine whether or not to continue with an action. Every **if** needs an **end**, to signify its completion.

6. **then** - Works after an **if** to pass on the actions, only if the **if** was successful.

7. **Texture** - Image reference in ROBLOX. Used on Decals, Meshes, and clothing.

8. **Giver** - When touched by a user it automatically adds a Tool.

9. **Tool** - A ROBLOX in-game item used by a user to interact with the environment.

Chapter 9

Player Assets and Properties

This is a brief chapter that gives a short description of the components of a Player.

In the game of ROBLOX every user is known as a Player, and every Player gets their life-like characteristics from a Humanoid. Along with this humanoid, when a Player is in a game they consist many properties to make them work both visually and physically.

Some of the components that make up a Player in a game cannot be seen. Plus, not all of these components are in the visible Workspace. Some of the components for a Player are in the Player Folder of a game. In the Player Folder are sub groupings for an individual Player. These are **StarterGear**, PlayerGUI, and **Backpack**. The StarterGear holds everything from the StarterPack that contains the gear a Player will respawn with. On the other hand, the Backpack contains all of the gear that a Player has at the current moment in their inventory.

A Humanoid is the most important part of a Player, but it is not the only important part. Inside of a Player are all of the body parts and textures to give the user its appearance. There are also scripts that give you your team, control your health, and make you animate while you move. Plus, every

Player contains **Sound**s that you hear as you walk, jump, or do any type of movement. Inside of all of these components are properties. Inside of the Player are the following Components:

Component	ClassName	Description
Body Colors	BodyColors	Sets Player's Brick colors
Shirt Graphic	ShirtGraphic	T-shirt graphic
Health	Script	Heals or Kills
HealthScript v3.1	Script	Manages Health GUI
Humanoid	Humanoid	Gives life-like characteristics
RobloxTeam	Script	Manages your team colors
Robloxclassicred	Hat	Sets your hat's appearance
Sound	Script	Plays sounds on movement
Animate	Script	Animates Character on action
Head	Brick	Head's appearance & face

Left Arm	Brick	Left Arm Brick
Left Leg	Brick	Left Leg Brick
Right Arm	Brick	Right Arm Brick
Right Leg	Brick	Right Leg Brick
Torso	Brick	Body connections & T-shirt

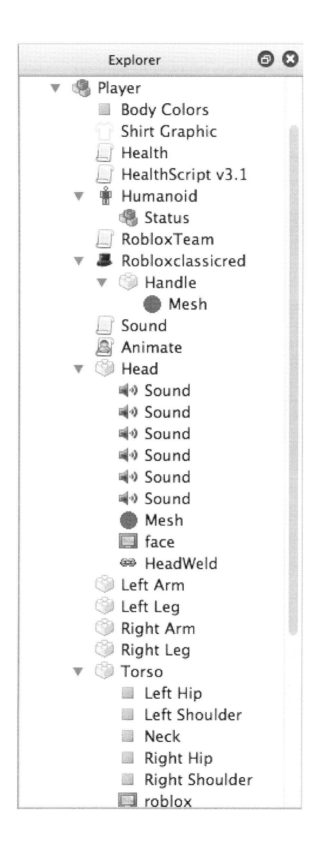

Overview – Player Assets and Properties

1. **StarterGear** - Holds everything from the StarterPack that contains the gear a Player will respawn with.

2. **Backpack** - Contains all of the gear that a Player has at the current moment in their inventory.

3. **Sound** - A noise that is played when an action occurs on ROBLOX.

Chapter 10

Tutorial 5 - Lava

In this chapter you will learn how to make a Brick or Part kill a user when touched.

In this chapter you will encounter a tutorial on creating **Lava**. Lava is the term used to describe a brick that kills a user when it is touched. Most of the time, as in real science, Lava is red. You can see uses of Lava on ROBLOX in games such as obstacle courses.

Within the scripting of the Lava for this tutorial you will be accessing the Humanoid of a player. As you access the Humanoid you will manipulate the health of a user. To begin our tutorial, you will need to create an Empty Baseplate game. Then, using ROBLOX Studio, go into the game with Edit Mode.

Once in the game we will add a basic Part from the Insert Panel of the File Bar:

Insert -> Object -> Part

Next, move the part away from its default position so you do not land on the killing brick when you **Spawn**. Then, highlight the brick in the Explorer and make sure that you can view the Property Panel. In the Part's properties, we can make the Lava more realistic. Click on the color property and chose a Red color. Also, click on the Material property and choose **Slate**.

Since we now have a part that will serve as the physical side of our Lava, we can add a Script. In the Explorer, highlight the Part and add a script from the Insert Panel in the File Bar:

Insert -> Object -> Script

Double-click this script in the Explorer to open it in the Script Editor.

Before editing the script with our own code, you now must clear the script. For the first line in our script we will declare our Part as a **local** named *Lava*. We create this reference to shorten the term script.Parent into one word:

local Lava = script.Parent -- Our Lava Part

Once again, this Lava reference will serve to handle physical interactions to find out when and who to kill.

After declaring our **local**, we must signal the beginning of our **function**. In this Script, our **function** must pass on a reference to the object that triggered the Touched event on **Lava**. Add the following line of code:

function onTouch(Brick) -- Sets the start of our function and when triggered it gives Brick, the object that was hit

As the reference to the trigger, we will be using Brick.

We now have our **function** declared and the trigger discovered our script must do some verifications. First, before committing any actions we need to search for a Humanoid, which is only present in a "living" user. To do this we will declare another **local** named as Player:

local Player =
Brick.Parent:findFirstChild("Humanoid") -- Looks for a Humanoid in Brick

Even though we have a declared **local** for a Humanoid, we still need to verify that it exists. If we do not verify that it exists, our script will crash when trying to access it. So, we will make sure that Player is not equal to **nil**. Use the following line in your script:

if (Player ~= **nil**) **then** -- Checks if Player is a real Player

Because we are comparing to the term **nil** with ~=
(not equal to) the **then** will not be passed unless
Player truly exists.

If all of our past events have triggered
successfully, we can finally work in the core
functionality of our code. In the core of the script
will be the killing code. There are many ways to kill
a Player, you can remove their vital parts (head,
torso), subtract health, or set their health to zero. In
this tutorial we will set the Humanoid health value
itself minus 100:

Player.Health = Player.Health - 100 -- Subtracts 100
Health from Player's Humanoid

On a Player's Humanoid, the **MaxHealth** Property is
100, so by subtracting 100 health we kill them.

This tutorial has a very short purpose, so we
can now declare the **end**s. We have one **function**
and an **if**. Let's add two **end**s:

end

end

All that is left in our script is to make a connection

between our **function** and the Touched event with Lava:

Lava.Touched:connect(onTouch) -- Connect function to Touched event

Finally, we can put all of the code together. The code will kill a real Player that touches it, by searching for a humanoid and changing the health property. You code should look like this:

local Lava = script.Parent -- Our Lava Part

function onTouch(Brick) -- Sets the start of our function and when triggered it gives Brick, the object that was hit

local Player = Brick.Parent:findFirstChild("Humanoid") -- Looks for a Humanoid in Brick

if (Player ~= **nil**) **then** -- Checks if Player is a real Player

Player.Health = Player.Health - 100 -- Subtracts 100 Health from Player's Humanoid

end

end

Lava.Touched:connect(onTouch) -- Connect function to Touched event

Your code is ready to test if it matches up correctly, so you can enter a Play Solo test by this shortcut in the File Bar:

Tools -> Test -> Play Solo

If your test is successful, your character will die on touch to the Lava. Return to the Game window to save and exit your game. You have completed this tutorial!

Overview – Lava

1. **Lava** - A Brick or Part that kills or damages a user who touches it.

2. **Spawn** - An object that a user comes back to life on or start the game on in ROBLOX. The act of coming back to life on ROBLOX.

3. **Slate** - A type of Material for a Brick or Part.

4. **MaxHealth** - The maximum or full health value for a Humanoid.

Chapter 11

Special Effect Components

This chapter will go into basic descriptions about visual and non-visual effects on ROBLOX.

The game of ROBLOX includes many different effects that you can add into a physical object. Some of these effects are just for show and some have influences on surrounding objects. None of these effects have any physical density and serve as an overlaying layer.

One of these harmless effects is **Sparkles**. Sparkles are like ROBLOX glitter, or fireworks. These appear as star shaped objects flying outwards from a brick. You can customize the color of Sparkles just like you can customize the color of a Brick or Part. Also, these have no effect on the environment.

A second effect is the **Forcefield**. A Forcefield is a special barrier around an object. Forcefields have been recently redesigned to a new appearance. Now, one component of a Forcefield's appearance is a sphere that slowly fades-in and fades-out. Another component of a Forcefield is sparkles that float upwards.

Third in the chapter is **Smoke**. This exactly what it is named, and appears as a smog-like overlaying smoke that blocks the view of distant objects. You can customize the color of smoke to create different effects such as water or fog.

Next, is the **Flames** effect. A flame flows like smoke in an upward velocity by default. This effect does damage to surrounding object with the wood **Material**. If this Flame touches a wooden Brick or Part, it will also catch on fire and burn until it turns to ash.

A different kind of effect is a **BillboardGUI**, which works off of GUIs. The concept of a BillboardGUI is a GUI that appears over a Brick or Part and rotates to increase/decrease in size as you come into range. BillboardGUIs can range from full capabilities of a GUI with the same basic components.

With a different aspect of effects, there is the audio **Sound** effect. A sound can be set to IsPaused or IsPlaying. Also, you can set a sound to be looped and repeat itself constantly. In the properties of a sound you can also change the Pitch and Volume.

Overview – Special Effect Components

1. **Sparkles -** Star shaped objects flying outwards from a brick.

2. **Forcefield -** A special barrier around an object.

3. **Smoke -** A smog-like overlaying smoke that blocks the view of distant objects.

4. **Flames -** Smoke-like fire that flows in an upward velocity by default.

5. **Material -** Texture and appearance of a Brick or Part, that also influences traits determining interactions with the environment (ex. Stone, wood).

6. **BilboardGUI -** A GUI that appears over a Brick or Part and rotates to increase/decrease in size as a user comes into range.

Chapter 12

Tutorial 6 – Hat Changer

In this chapter you will find out how to make a script that will change the current appearance of a user's hat that touches a Part.

By reading this tutorial you will start to put your knowledge from *Player Asset and Properties* into use. You will be manipulating the **Hat**'s appearance of a user who touches a Part that contains our script. Also, you will learn how to search the Children of a Model or Group.

To start this tutorial you will need to go into an Empty Baseplate using ROBLOX Studio in Edit Mode. Then, you will need to add a Part from the Insert Panel accessible from the File Bar:

Insert -> Object -> Part

Also, you will have to add a script into the Part that you just added. To add a script you will also be using the Insert Panel after highlighting your Part in the Explorer. Insert a script into your part:

Insert -> Object -> Script

You will not be required to change the size of this Part, but it may help if you move it a few studs from where it is automatically inserted. If you choose not to move the Part, it will be an inconvenience because when you go into Play Solo, you will spawn directly above the Part.

First, you can double-click on the script to open it in a Script Editor. As the first line of your script we will add our first **local** declaration to reference our Part that Parents the Script. Let's name this **local** as *Morpher*.

local Morpher = script.Parent -- Declare the Part as Morpher

We will not find ourselves using this reference much throughout the tutorial, but it is always helpful to define a **local** for script.Parent.

Next, we will mark the start of our **function**. In this Script our **function** will pass us the object that triggers our Touched event. It is fairly simple to do this, as we have done it before in a previous tutorial:

function onTouch(Brick) -- Sets the start of our function and when triggered it gives Brick, the object that was hit

The third thing that we will now do is search for the children of Brick.Parent. When we do this we will be creating a **Programmatic Table** with references to the components of Brick.Parent which hopefully will be a Player. To get the children we will be using a :GetChildren() call. After marking the start to your **function**, add the following line to your script:

```
for item, child in pairs(Brick.Parent:GetChildren())
do -- Searches Player and creates a table => item
      is row number in table, and child is object
```

Above, we are creating two **Column**s in a table. One column is item which is the **Row** number of child, the second column, which is the component of our Player being referenced. By using **for** and **do** we will be doing the proceeding code for every child. A side note is that every **for** requires an **end**.

Now, after making a programatic table of the components of our player, we will search for the Hat. In order to find our Hat, we will search based on the ClassName. We have to search by ClassName because the Name of every Hat is based on the Name of the Hat in the ROBLOX Catalog. This is going to be referencing to the child column in our table:

```
if child.ClassName == 'Hat' then -- Only changes
      object with the ClassName of Hat
```

The **then** will be initiating the code that follows only to a Hat.

Finally, we can now make the changes to the Hat of the Player. In the script we will change the Name, Mesh, and Texture of the Hat. For this tutorial I will be using the properties of a Hat known as *Bloxxer Cap*. I will bundle all of the changes below:

child.Name = "Cap" -- Rename Hat

child.Handle.Mesh.MeshId = "http://www.roblox.com/asset/?id=16190466" -- Change the Mesh of the Hat

child.Handle.Mesh.TextureId = "http://www.roblox.com/asset/?id=51278992" -- Change the Texture of the Hat

In a Hat, the **Handle** is the physical brick which contains the Mesh.

One of the last things we need to do is make signal an **end** to our **function, for**, and **if**. We will only need to add three **end**s:

end

end

end

Lastly we must make a touch connection between **Morpher** and the **function**. This is the only time we have needed to reference **Morpher** in our script:

Morpher.Touched:connect(onTouch) -- Connect function to Touched event

Make sure that all of your code matches up to the following:

local Morpher = script.Parent -- Declare the Part as Morpher

function onTouch(Brick) -- Sets the start of our function and when triggered it gives Brick, the object that was hit

for item, child **in** pairs(Brick.Parent:GetChildren()) **do** -- Searches Player and creates a table => item is row number in table, and child is object

if child.ClassName == 'Hat' **then** -- Only changes object with the ClassName of Hat

```
child.Name = "Cap" -- Rename Hat

child.Handle.Mesh.MeshId =
"http://www.roblox.com/asset/?id=16190466" --
Change the Mesh of the Hat

child.Handle.Mesh.TextureId =
"http://www.roblox.com/asset/?id=51278992" --
Change the Texture of the Hat

end

end

end

Morpher.Touched:connect(onTouch) -- Connect
function to Touched event
```

If everything matches up correctly, you may test the game in Play Solo. To go into Play Solo use this shortcut in the File Bar:

Tools -> Test -> Play Solo

Your game will work correctly if the hat changes to a white *Bloxxer Cap*. Now you can go back into the Game Window to save and exit. You have successfully completed this tutorial.

Overview – Hat Changer

1. **Hat** - Object worn on the Head of a Player.

2. **Programmatic Table** - A non-visual table created solely for the use of a script.

3. **Column** - Vertical segment of a table.

4. **Row** - Horizontal segment of a table.

5. **for** - A call that passes the proceeding code based upon a series of objects.

6. **do** - Passes the content of a **for** call.

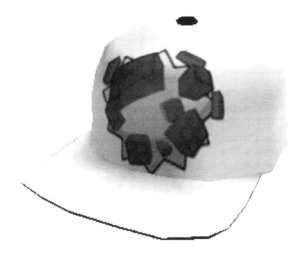

Chapter 13

Basics of CFrame

In this chapter you will be introduced to the concepts of CFrame.

In this chapter you will lean about the concepts of **CFrame**. The term CFrame stands for Coordinate Frame and represents the position and rotation of a Part or Brick.

In a mathematical view of CFrame, the rotational properties can form a **Matrix**. These Matrices are based on the X, Y, and Z axes. In ROBLOX the format of a location in Lua is (X, Y, Z). For example, if you were to try to move a Part up 5 studs you would use the following:

$$Part.CFrame = CFrame.new(0, 5, 0)$$

Which as a matrix would look like:

$$|0|$$

$$|5|$$

$$|0|$$

To talk about this matrix you would indicate the number by its spot in the matrix. A number in matrix has a location based upon rows and columns. Visually you would refer to the location using a variable like this (different than mathematical format):

|R00 R01 R02|

|R10 R11 R12|

|R20 R21 R22|

However, back to the concept of CFrame, every time you want to change the CFrame of a brick you declare a new **Constructor**. A constructor acts as a new instance for a location. So when setting Part.CFrame = CFrame.new it sets the CFrame of **Part** to the CFrame.new.

Also paired with CFrame is **Vector3**, which represents the 3D location of an object. We could use Vector3 to set something like this:

Part.CFrame =
CFrame.new(Part2.Position+Vector3.new(0, 5, 0))

In this example, we set the CFrame location of **Part** with Vector3 to 5 studs higher on the y-axis than the position of **Part2**. Using +Vector3 performing a slide transformation.

Plus, in the properties of CFrame, you can fetch the CFrame value from an object. These values are read-only and cannot be edited. It is because of the read-only capabilities that we create a new Constructor every time we change the CFrame of an object. You can load the CFrame value of an object based on the table below:

Property	Type	Description
CFrame.p	Vector3	The 3D position of the CFrame
CFrame.x	Number	the x-component of the Vector3 position
CFrame.y	Number	the y-component of the Vector3 position
CFrame.z	Number	the z-component of the Vector3 position
CFrame.lookVector	Vector3	returns the facing direction (unit vector)

For example, you can print the CFrame value into the Output like such:

```
print("CFrame Value:" .. Part.Cframe.x)
```

In the code above we would display the x-axis CFrame location.

These are the basics that will be covered in this tutorial. CFrame can be much more complex with rotational axes. For more you can go to (http://wiki.roblox.com/index.php/CFrame).

Overview – Basics of CFrame

---

1. **CFrame -** Stands for Coordinate Frame and represents the positioning and rotation of a Part or Brick.

2. **Matrix -** A mathematical array of geometric and 3D coordinates.

3. **Constructor -** A new instance of a CFrame position.

4. **Vector3 -** Movement of an object by sliding.

Chapter 14

Tutorial 7 - Teleporter

In this chapter you will learn how to make a Brick or Part instantly move a Player to the location or another Brick or Part.

As of right now, it's very slow to just walk around a whole map on ROBLOX. We should make this process faster. In order to speed things up we will create a **Teleporter**. A Teleporter will instantly move our Character from one location to another. In this case, we will be moving the Character from one Part that they touch, to another.

Let's start by going into an Empty Baseplate in ROBLOX Studio in Edit Mode. As usual we will will be using a Part as the holder for our script. However, this time we will need to add two Parts. One of these parts will be the **Trigger** and the other will be the **Receiver**. Add a Part with through this shortcut in the File Bar, but do it twice:

Insert -> Object -> Part

Automatically the Parts should have been placed on top of one another. For better results in this tutorial you should space the two Parts apart from each other. Since we will be using multiple Parts, we can **Group** them into a **Model**. Highlight both of these Parts in the Explorer, then right-click on them and hit *Group* or hit the keys *control+g*. By grouping these Parts together it makes it easier for them to find each other in in the clutter of a Workspace. Now, rename the new Group as *Teleporter* and one of the Parts *T1* and the other as *T2*. Click on the Part that you just named *T1* and insert a Script into it using the File Bar:

Insert -> Object -> Script

Okay, now that you have the components set up in your game you can begin scripting. Double-click on the newly added script in *T1* to open it in the Script Editor. Once you have opened it in the Script Editor, clear the script.

We will start by defining *T1* and *T2* in **local** declarations. The first two lines of code in your script will read the following:

local Tel1 = script.Parent -- Our Parenting Part

local Tel2 = script.Parent.Parent.T2 -- The part we will teleport to

All we are doing here is making a one-word reference to the two Parts we will be teleporting to and from.

Next, we will kick off the **function** that will tell

us the object to teleport. Enter the following code:

function onTouch(Brick) -- Starts the function that sends us Brick, the object that triggers the function

When an object triggers this **function**, it will let us know what it is by passing itself as **Brick**.

   After finding out **Brick** we will need to do work to make sure that it is an actual user trying to be teleported. To do this, we will search **Brick** for a Humanoid. We will use a **local** declaration to verify later. Use the following code:

local Player = Brick.Parent:findFirstChild("Humanoid") -- Finds Humanoid in Brick

After declaring a **local** that we can verify as a Humanoid, we will need to actually write the code to use as verification. To do this we will be using **if** and **then** functions. You might recognize some of this code from previous tutorials:

if (Player ~= **nil**) **then** -- Checks if Player is a real Player

If the **Player** is a real user with a valid Humanoid,

we use **then** to continue.

Finally we have done enough tests to validate that we are teleporting a real user. So now we can code the teleporting part of our script. The method that we will be using will be CFrame based off of the position of Tel2. If we did not use CFrame to move the Torso of our Player, the body would break connections and kill the Player. This code is lengthy, but serves our purpose perfectly:

Player.Parent.Torso.CFrame = CFrame.new(Tel2.Position+Vector3.new(0, 3, 0)) -- Moves Player to the teleporter, but up three studs higher

Above, the code simply CFrames Player's Torso to the position of Tel2 but up 3 studs higher on the x-axis. By moving the Player up we counteract the size of the Torso and Legs so that the Player appears directly on top of Tel2.

Lastly, we can call an **end** to everything we have left open. In this script we will need an **end** for our **function** and **if**. Let's add two **end**s.

end

end

All that is left to do is make the connection between Tel1 being touched and our **function**. In the beginning of our script we already defined Tel1 so we can just add the following code to out script:

```
Tel1.Touched:connect(onTouch) -- Connect the
function to a touched event
```

In the end your code should read this:

```
local Tel1 = script.Parent -- Our Parenting Part
```

```
local Tel2 = script.Parent.Parent.T2 -- The part we
will teleport to
```

```
function onTouch(Brick) -- Starts the function that
sends us Brick, the object that triggers the function
```

```
local Player =
Brick.Parent:findFirstChild("Humanoid") -- Finds
Humanoid in Brick
```

```
if (Player ~= nil) then -- Checks if Player is a real
Player
```

```
    Player.Parent.Torso.CFrame =
CFrame.new(Tel2.Position+Vector3.new(0, 3, 0)) --
Moves Player to the teleporter, but up three studs
                    higher

                     end

                     end

    Tel1.Touched:connect(onTouch) -- Connect the
            function to a touched event
```

Return to the Game Window to save and exit. Then, go back into the game in Edit Mode of ROBLOX Studio. Our script is ready for testing. Use the File Bar to go into Play Solo:

Tools -> Test -> Play Solo

When your testing, if you are teleported from **Tel1** to **Tel2** your Script is successful. However, if your Script was not successful, just make sure you copied down all of the code correctly.

Again you may return to the Game Window to

save and exit. You have successfully completed
this tutorial!

Overview – Teleporter

1. **Teleporter -** A Part that moves a user from one location to another instantaneously.

2. **Trigger -** Object that sends an action.

3. **Receiver -** Object that receives an action.

4. **Group -** Multiple Parts contained in the same Model, under one Parent.

5. **Model -** A grouping of Parts that are brought together by the same Parent.

Chapter 15

Working With Strings

In this chapter you will learn about string manipulations.

In this chapter you will find out how to set and manipulate **String**s. A String is a basic text value used to define any text property such as an item's Name. Also, you will find out how to print a String into the Output. For all instances of defining a String, we will be creating a **local**.

ROBLOX allows many different ways by which to create a String, and they all serve a different purpose. The most common type of String uses "" around the text. You can do this like the following:

local String = "Hello"

Also, you can do the same with single quotes '', which can also be used to have a quote in a string. To demonstrate both of these techniques:

local String = 'The Man said, "Hello" today'

Then, you can view your results by making it print in the Output. By making it print, when your Script runs it will display as a result. It is very helpful to use print functionalities when you have a long Script. If we were to print the **String** above we would use:

print (String)

Another way to go about this is by directly stating the String to print:

print ("Hello")

Using this same simple "" stated String we can merge two Strings with two ".." in the middle. We could use this method with:

local String = "Hello" .. "!"

This can be helpful to also merge a preset String with a value that is undefined until your script is ran; This could be any value such as a certain User's name.

Another method to define a string uses two brackets [[ ]]. These brackets will serve as quotation marks. Use them like this:

local String = [[Hello]]

Within a String there can be multiple lines. To add multiple lines in your string with "", a backslash (\) is used. For example:

local String = "One\Two\Three"

In the Output this would display as:

One

Two

Three

On the other hand, if you were using a String created in [ ] you would just enter to a new line.

There is one inconvenience about a String. Since a String is a text value, it will not natively take the place of an **Integer** or number value. For us to be able to use a String for an integer, we need to get the number value from the String. We can use the following on any String:

local String = "100"

local Number = tonumber(String)

With this **function** you are not able to convert any other Strings than a number-only String. If you try to convert a String that says "Hello" it will return as invalid.

Strings have many complicated symbols that can be alternated to change the context, and many of the ways shown in this tutorial can be combined.

Overview – Working With Strings

---

1. **String** - A basic text value used to define any property with text.

2. **Integer** - A number value. (ex. 100)

Chapter 16

Tutorial 8 – Random Number Humanoid

In this tutorial we will use a Humanoid and our knowledge of Strings combined with math to create a random number generator when a button is Clicked.

In this tutorial we will learn how to correctly utilize a Humanoid to display text above a Brick or Part. In utilizing a Humanoid you will be told about the proper grouping and naming that is needed. You will also learn about **Math** functions. Math functions relate to the basic use of integers in correspondence with each other. Lastly, you will face your first time using a **ClickDetector** to detect a click on a Brick or Part to trigger a **function**. ClickDetectors do not natively come inside of a Brick or Part; you must insert them just like a script.

To begin, go into an Empty Baseplate in ROBLOX Studio in Edit Mode. First we will add an empty Model through the File Bar:

Insert -> Object -> Model

This empty Model will serve as the container for our Humanoid and Part. Every Humanoid must be inside a Model that has a corresponding Part named *Head*. The name of the Model determines the Text displayed by the Humanoid. Insert a Humanoid from the File Bar directly into our new Model:

Insert -> Object -> Humanoid

Add a Part from the File Bar into the Model, then name it *Head*:

Insert -> Object -> Part

Also, add a Script from the File Bar into our Part:

Insert -> Object -> Script

Now we will need to add a ClickDetector into our Part. A ClickDetector is also available in the File Bar:

Insert -> Object -> ClickDetector

This is all that we will need to add.

Let us start of by double-clicking on our Script in the Explorer to open the Script Editor. After the Script Editor is open, you may clear the Script. As the first line in the Script, we will declare a **local** for our Part named *Head* and another **local** for our Model named *Model*:

local Head = script.Parent -- Our Part named Head

local Model = script.Parent.Parent -- The Model containing the Part

After defining our **local**s we will mark the beginning of the **function**. Since this will be a click **function**, we will name it differently. Names do not matter for **function**s as long as it corresponds to the connection you make at the end of a script. For our **function** add this code:

function onClick() -- Start function

Inside of our **function** we will now do some math to determine multiple random numbers. In this tutorial I am going to generate five random numbers (1-9) for individual digits in the number that we will display on the Humanoid. You could also just generate a random number with a larger range, and only need to go it once. For ROBLOX, you kick off a math call with **math**. In our case, we will be using the **random**() instance of **math**. Inside of the () for **random** will be two numbers, these numbers declare the range that the random number will be in. Here is what we will be using, and they will be declared as five **local**s:

local Num1 = **math. random**(1, 9) -- Random Number

local Num2 = **math. random**(1, 9) -- Random

Number

local Num3 = **math**. **random**(1, 9) -- Random
Number

local Num4 = **math**. **random**(1, 9) -- Random
Number

local Num5 = **math**. **random**(1, 9) -- Random
Number

Using our newly generated numbers, we need to create a combined five digit number. To merge the numbers together, we can use the same method as we do to merge strings:

local Number = Num1 .. Num2 .. Num3 .. Num4 ..
Num5 -- Combine Numbers

We will now take this **local** to set the Text to be displayed on our Humanoid. The text will be determined by the name of *Model*, so that is what we will change:

Model.Name = Number -- Set Number to display as
Humanoid Name

Finally we can **end** our **function**:

end

Below the **end** will be our final connection of the Click event and our **function**:

Head.ClickDetector.MouseClick:connect(onClick) -- Connect Click Event on ClickDetector in Head with function

To detect a click on a Click detector, we simple search for a **MouseClick** action.

Before we go ahead, make sure that you have entered all of the correct code. Together all of your code should be the following:

local Head = script.Parent -- Our Part named Head

local Model = script.Parent.Parent -- The Model containing the Part

function onClick() -- Start function

local Num1 = **math. random**(1, 9) -- Random Number

local Num2 = **math. random**(1, 9) -- Random

Number

local Num3 = **math. random**(1, 9) -- Random
Number

local Num4 = **math. random**(1, 9) -- Random
Number

local Num5 = **math. random**(1, 9) -- Random
Number

local Number = Num1 .. Num2 .. Num3 .. Num4 ..
Num5 -- Combine Numbers

Model.Name = Number -- Set Number to display as
Humanoid Name

end

Head.ClickDetector.MouseClick:connect(onClick) --
Connect Click Event on ClickDetector in Head with
function

If all of your code matches up, you can go back to
the Game window to save and exit your game.
Then, re-enter your game in Edit Mode of ROBLOX
Studio. Go into a Play Solo Test in the File Bar:

Tools -> Test -> Play Solo

In the test, you will know if you game works correctly if a new number is generated above the Part every time you click it. Tutorial complete!

Overview – Random Number Humanoid

1. **Math** - Mathematical interactions between integers - numerical values.

2. **ClickDetector** - Detects a click on a Brick or Part to trigger a **function**.

3. **math** - A call that marks the beginning of a mathematical function.

4. **random**() - Subclass of a math call to generate a random number between a certain range.

Chapter 17

Script Functions and Methods

In this chapter you will be introduced to different functions and services in a ROBLOX script.

This chapter will go over the basic **Function**s and **Method**s to be called in a script. Here is a table that will be followed by brief descriptions:

Type	Method/ Function	Explanation
Function	delay()	Sets time before a **function** is executed. **Example:** delay(2, **function**() -- Stuff **end**)
Function	wait()	Makes a script pause before continuing. **Example:** wait(2)
Method	:Clone()	Duplicates an object. **Example:** script.Parent:Clone()
Method	:FindFirstChild()	Finds objects by ClassName. **Example:** **local** User = script.Parent:findFirstChild ("Humanoid")
Method	:GetChildren()	Grabs all Children of an object. **Example:** **for** item, child **in** pairs(script.Parent:GetChildren()) **do**
Method	:Remove()	Deletes an item.

		Example: script.Parent:Remove()
Method	:Destroy()	Completely Removes all memory and connections to an object. **Example:** script.Parent:Destroy()
Method	:MakeJoints()	Makes a bond between touching Bricks or Parts that have appropriately corresponding Surface types. **Example:** script.Parent:MakeJoints()
Method	:BreakJoints()	Removes bonds between touching objects. **Example:** script.Parent:BreakJoints()
Method	:GetMass()	The non-editable mass of a Brick or Part. **Example:** script.Parent:GetMass()
Method	:BreakJoints()	Removes bonds between touching objects. **Example:** script.Parent:BreakJoints()
Method	:MoveTo()	Moves object to a new location. **Example:** script.Parent:MoveTo(Vector3. new(0, 10, 20))

Overview – Script Functions and Methods

1. **Function** - Built in calls to a script.

2. **Method** - Useful services beginning with a : and ending with an ().

Chapter 18

Tutorial 9 – Click Clone

In this chapter you will read about how to Clone a Part and assign it a name using upon math.

This tutorial will teach how to duplicate a Part then manipulate its physical location in the game. Also you will assign the Part a Random Color. Lastly you will use math to rename the Part based upon the number of times the Script has ran.

Kick-off the tutorial by opening a new Empty Baseplate and entering it through Edit Mode of ROBLOX Studio. The first component that will be added to this game is a Part from the File Bar:

Insert -> Object -> Part

Into this Part we must first add a ClickDetector to later detect a **MouseClick** event.

Insert -> Object -> ClickDetector

Secondly, we will add an **IntValue** object from the File Bar. An IntValue is an object with a editable **Number Value**.

Insert -> Object -> IntValue

Also, we need to add a Script from the File Bar:

Insert -> Object -> Script

On the Script that was just added, highlight and

double-click it in the Explorer to open the Script Editor. Clear the Script before we begin. On the first two lines of our Script we will define two **local** references. One **local** will be for our Part named *Target*, and the other will be for our Value named *Num*. Enter the following code into your Script:

```
local Target = script.Parent -- Our Part
```

```
local Num = script.Parent.Value -- Our IntValue
```

Next, we will begin our **function**. This will be for a Click event. We will make the connection at the end of our script as usual. Here is the code:

```
function onClick() -- Start function
```

In the core of our Script we will first define a **local** for the Clone of our Part. Name the **local** as *Clone*:

```
local Clone = Target:Clone () -- Duplicate of Target
```

Now, that we have a Clone of our Part there needs to be changes made. First we will re-position Clone:

```
Clone.Cframe = Cframe.new(Target.Position) --
```

Change position of Clone to the position of Target

Then, we will change the Name of **Clone** by working with **Num**. The Script will set the Name to include the **Value** of **Num**. After using **Num** once the Script will increase the Value of **Num**. Use these two lines of code:

Clone.Name = "Clone" .. Num.Value -- Change the
Name of Clone to include the Value of Num

Num.Value = Num.Value + 1 -- Increase the Value
of Num by 1

After that, we will set the Color of **Clone** to a Random Color with this code:

Clone.BrickColor = BrickColor.Random() -- Change
the Color of Clone to a random Color

Finally, now that all of the changes have been made to **Clone**, it can now be placed into the game. Insert the **Clone** into the game's Workspace:

Clone.Parent = game.Workspace -- Insert Clone
into the Workspace

Lastly, we have to **end** the **function**. We only

have one thing to mark an **end** to:

end

As the last line in our Script we will put the connection between our Part, **Target**, having a MouseClick event from the ClickDetector with our **function**.

Target.ClickDetector.MouseClick:connect(onClick) - - Connect Click Event on ClickDetector in Target with function

Verify that your code looks like the following, this is the overall code:

local Target = script.Parent -- Our Part

local Num = script.Parent.Value -- Our IntValue

function onClick() -- Start function

local Clone = Target:Clone () -- Duplicate of Target

Clone.Cframe = Cframe.new(Target.Position) -- Change position of Clone to the position of Target

Clone.Name = "Clone" .. Num.Value -- Change the

Name of Clone to include the Value of Num

Num.Value = Num.Value + 1 -- Increase the Value of Num by 1

Clone.BrickColor = BrickColor:Random() -- Change the Color of Clone to a random Color

Clone.Parent = game.Workspace -- Insert Clone into the Workspace

end

Target.ClickDetector.MouseClick:connect(onClick) -- Connect Click Event on ClickDetector in Target with function

Return to the Game Window to save and exit your game. Then, return to the game in Edit Mode of ROBLOX Studio. Go into a Play Solo test in the File Bar:

Tools -> Test -> Play Solo

In the test, observe that the tutorial has been successful if a new Brick appears to our specifications when you Click the main Part. After Cloning the main Part once, you will also be able to

Clone the duplicates, this is because it contains the same components. Return to the Game Window to save and exit your game. Tutorial Successful!

Overview – Click Clone

1. **MouseClick -** An event when a ClickDetector is clicked by a User to trigger a **function**.

2. **Value -** A numerical property of certain objects.

Chapter 19

Starterpack, Backpack, and Tools

This chapter will be a very short chapter explaining the difference of the uses between the StarterPack, Backpack, and Tools.

In a ROBLOX game, a **Tool** is a term that refers to an item which a User uses to interact with the environment. Tools are referred to as Gear, and can either be unique to a game or bought in the ROBLOX Catalog. There are many different types of tools to categorize the different ways that they can be used, such as transportation or melee. Different categories will also be used to organize which Tools are allowed into different games.

Games have different groupings to organize Tools based upon how often a User will receive them. If a User is meant to receive a Tool every time they respawn in the game, it will be placed into the game's **StarterPack**. A StarterPack is one of a kind, and has only one instance in a game. Everything in the StarterPack will be distributed the same way to every User.

One level ahead of the StarterPack is the Backpack. The Backpack is a grouping in a game that includes all of the current Gear of a User. If a game directly inserts a Tool into the Backpack of a User, they will lose it when they die.

This is a very short Chapter. It serves to solely get the basic levels of Tools in ROBLOX across.

Overview – Starterpack, Backpack, and Tools

1. **Tools -** An item, which a User uses to interact with the environment.

2. **StarterPack -** Location for all permanent Tools in a game to be placed, which any User will always receive when they spawn.

3. **BackPack -** A grouping, which holds the current Tools of a User.

Chapter 20

Tutorial 10 - Giver

In this tutorial you will learn how to Insert a Tool into a Player's backpack once they touch a Brick or Part.

In this tutorial you will learn how to give a User a Tool when they touch a Brick or Part. We will be inserting a Tool using a Clone method. The Tool will be inserted into the Player's Backpack, so they will lose it upon death. In doing this tutorial, you will find out how to retrieve the Player's location in the Player folder from their Character in the Workspace.

The object that we will be creating is known as a Giver. A Giver can be any object that dispenses an object to a user, or automatically inserts it into their Backpack. Most Givers are used to grant optional Gear, or give Tools to a limited number of Users.

Start by going into an Empty Baseplate in Edit Mode of ROBLOX Studio. First, we need to insert a Part into our game through the File Bar:

Insert -> Object -> Part

Next, add a Script into this Part after highlighting it in the Explorer:

Insert -> Object -> Script

Inside of our Part we also need the Tool that we will be giving the User. You can find the Tool object in the File Bar. To start the Tool will have no functionality, but that is all we need in this tutorial:

Insert -> Object -> Tool

Once we have all of our physical components inserted into the game, double-click the Script in the Explorer to open the Script Editor. Clear the new Script so we can begin to add our own content. As the first **local** for our code, we will define our Part as *Giver*:

local Giver = script.Parent -- Our Part

Then, we will define a reference to our Tool as a **local** named *Gear*:

local Gear = script.Parent.Tool -- The Tool to give

Secondly, we will mark the beginning of our **function**. In this tutorial, the **function** will pass us the triggering object just as seen in previous tutorials. This trigger will be referenced to by the name of *Brick*. Add this code to your Script:

function onTouch(Brick) -- Start the function to pass us the triggering object as Brick

As the first line after our f **function** we need to use **Brick** to search for a Humanoid, which only exists in a real Player. We will declare this in a **local** named *Player*. You have seen this before in an earlier tutorial:

local Player =
Brick.Parent:findFirstChild("Humanoid") -- Search
for a Humanoid

With this **local** we must verify that it is in existence and truly is referring to a real User. To do this we will use an **if** and **then** function:

if (Player ~= **nil**) **then** -- Verify that the Humanoid in
Player exists

All of the initializing of our script is done, so now it is time to code the core of our Script. First in this part of our code we need to define a **local** to reference the Player's Folder in the Players Grouping of the game, as is visible in the Explorer. To do this the script will use a service to fetch the Player's Folder, which corresponds with their Character. Use the following code to name a **local** as *Location*:

```
local Location =
```
game:GetService('Players'):GetPlayerFromCharact
er(Player.Parent) -- Find Player folder for our Player

Also, there will have to be a **local** for the Clone of our Tool, and it will be named *New*. Instead of directly giving the Player the one Tool we have, we can duplicate it so that the Script can run numerous times. We do this with the following code:

```
local New = Gear:Clone()
```

The last thing in our core will be a relocation of our Tool's Clone named **New** into the Player's Backpack:

```
New.Parent = Location.Backpack -- Insert the
    duplicate of Tool into the Player's Backpack
```

Finally we can mark an **end** to the one **function** and the one **if**:

end

end

Lastly, after our **end**s there has to be a connection between a Touched event on *Giver* and the

function:

Giver.Touched:connect(onTouch) -- Connect a
Touched event to our function

All of the code in our Script is done. Before
continuing, please verify that your code matches the
overall code below:

local Giver = script.Parent -- Our Part

local Gear = script.Parent.Tool -- The Tool to give

function onTouch(Brick) -- Start the function to
pass us the triggering object as Brick

local Player =
Brick.Parent:findFirstChild("Humanoid") -- Search
for a Humanoid

if (Player ~= **nil**) **then** -- Verify that the Humanoid in
Player exists

local Location =
game:GetService('Players'):GetPlayerFromCharact
er(Player.Parent) -- Find Player folder for our Player

local New = Gear:Clone()

```lua
    New.Parent = Location.Backpack -- Insert the
    duplicate of Tool into the Player's Backpack

end

end

Giver.Touched:connect(onTouch) -- Connect a
    Touched event to our function
```

If everything matches up correctly, return to the Game Window to save and exit. Next, return to the game in Edit Mode of ROBLOX Studio. At last we can go into a Play Solo test through the File Bar:

Tools -> Test -> Play Solo

As you are in Play Solo you can see if the game works correctly if you are given a Tool upon interaction with our Part. Return to the Game Window to save and exit. Tutorial Complete.

Overview – Giver

1. game:GetService('Players'):GetPlayerFromCharacter() - A service which finds the corresponding Player Folder from a Character.

Chapter 21

ROBLOX
User GUIs

This chapter will teach the basic uses and types of ROBLOX User GUIs.

GUIs are the graphical components for the interface of any game. ROBLOX allows Users to manipulate onscreen GUIs. On ROBLOX, a GUI will come in the form of these components:

View	Description
ScreenGUI	The Container for a GUI
Frame	Basic GUI which is displayed as a plain box
ImageLabel	A Decal displaying GUI that allows for optional overlaying text
ImageButton	An interactive Decal displaying GUI button
TextLabel	A GUI box that displays text
TextButton	An interactive GUI button which displays text
BillboardGUI	A GUI container that appears above an object

In order for a GUI to display it will be inside of a ScreenGUI object, which can be placed in the StarterGUI. Any GUI inside of the StarterGUI will be given to the PlayerGUI of every user and therefore displayed on every Player's screen.

A StarterGUI will appear as a 2D overlay on the

screen of the User. In order for a GUI to be displayed, the **Visible** Property must be enabled.

If a GUI is meant to appear at a movable position in the game, it must be placed in a BillboardGUI in an object. A BillboardGUI is a substitute for a ScreenGUI. In a game a Billboard GUI will appear at a set position in relation to a Parenting object. This kind of GUI will rotate and resize itself with the distance and angle that a User is viewing it from. Games use GUIs to add enhanced features without the physical clutter. Some games are solely comprised of a GUI overlaying the screen in the form of an interactive 2D game.

Overview – ROBLOX User GUIs

1. **Visible** Property - If enabled, a GUI will become visible on the screen of a User.

Chapter 22

Tutorial 11 – GUI Appear Button

This tutorial will teach how to create a Button that creates and displays a GUI when clicked.

With this chapter you will learn how to create a GUI programmatically in a Script. Then you will find the Player's PlayerGUI folder. In the PlayerGUI folder you will be able to add your GUI to be displayed on the screen of the User. By programmatically creating a GUI you will learn basic ways of customizing a TextLabel GUI.

Go into an Empty Baseplate in Edit Mode of ROBLOX Studio. As the first component we will use a Part. This Script will work off of a Touched action, so no ClickDetector will be needed. Add the Part from the File Bar:

Insert -> Object -> Part

Into this Part we must add the Script that we will be using from the File Bar, make sure that you highlight the Part in the Explorer first:

Insert -> Object -> Script

Next, double-click on the newly added Script in the Explorer to open the Script Editor. Clear out the default contents of the Script so we may begin on a clean slate.

As the first action of our Script we will define

our Part as a **local** named *Button*.

local Button = script.Parent -- Our Part

After this, the start of our **function** will have to be marked. Do this just as any other Touched event:

function onTouch(Brick) -- Start the function to pass us the triggering object as Brick

Inside of the Script's **function** there will be a lot of core work and many **local** declarations. The first of these will search for a Humanoid in our Brick triggering object. You have seen this before, so I will also give the code to verify the Humanoid is in existence here:

local Player =
Brick.Parent:findFirstChild("Humanoid") -- Search for a Humanoid

if (Player ~= **nil**) **then** -- Verify that the Humanoid in Player Exists

If the **if** passes to **then** our script will continue.

When our Script continues, we will begin the sole **function**s of the Script, which work to create a

GUI and its necessities. To begin, we will define a **local** for the ScreenGUI, which will eventually hold our GUI.

local Holder = Instance.new("ScreenGui") -- Create a new ScreenGui to hold our GUI

To go with this ScreenGUI we are going to be defining a **local** for a TextLabel GUI. Eventually, this will be inserted into the ScreenGUI, but for now we need to create a new Instance:

local Label = Instance.new("TextLabel") -- Create a new GUI Label to be in our Holder

Both of these components must be eventually added into the PlayerGUI of our Player. In order to find this we will use a method to retrieve the Player Folder in the Players location of the game. This is the same location as the Backpack of a User. Here is how to go about finding the Player Folder:

local Location = game:GetService('Players'):GetPlayerFromCharacter(Player.Parent) -- Find Player folder for our Player

All of the **local**s have now been declared for our script.

With the three new **local**s we can organize and setup the properties and locations of the new GUI. As the initial step, the Script will first position the GUI components in the game. Our **Holder** will be added into the PlayerGUI and the **Label** into **Holder**. Add these two lines of code:

Holder.Parent = Location.PlayerGUI -- Insert the Holder into the PlayerGUI

Label.Parent = Holder -- Insert our Label into the Holder

Once our **Label** has a proper location in the game, we can configure the GUI's onscreen appearance. We will set the Label's **GUI Text** to include our Player's Name. Then, we will position the Label on the screen and define the physical 2D size. Last, we will configure the **GUI Text Font** and **GUI Text Size**. Fonts for a GUI are limited and can be seen in the Property Panel. This jumble for code is the following, and takes up five lines:

Label.Text = "Hello " .. Player.Parent.Name -- Set the text of our Label and include the Player's name

Label.Position = UDim2.new(0, 100, 0, 100) --

Position the Label

Label.Size = UDim2.new(0, 100, 0, 100) -- Position
the Label

Label.Font = "ArialBold" -- Change the font of the
Label

Label.FontSize = "Size14" -- Change the font size
of the Label

GUI **Position** and **Size** works off of **UDim2** which corresponds with the Parenting GUI. For a GUI the 0 position is the Top Left of a GUI. A **UDim2** would look like this:

(xScale, xOffset, yScale, yOffset)

As we have just finished the code for the Script's only **function**, it is time to signal a few **end**s. The **end**s to be marked will be for our **function** and **if**. Here you go:

end

end

At last, the final line of our Script is ready. Following the two **end**s, the Touched event between our Part and **function** needs to be connected:

Button.Touched:connect(onTouch) -- Connect a Touched event on the Part to our function

All of the code that will be in our Script is done, so you should verify that everything has been entered correctly. The whole Script should appear as follows:

local Button = script.Parent -- Our Part

function onTouch(Brick) -- Start the function to pass us the triggering object as Brick

local Player = Brick.Parent:findFirstChild("Humanoid") -- Search for a Humanoid

if (Player ~= **nil**) **then** -- Verify that the Humanoid in Player Exists

local Holder = Instance.new("ScreenGui") -- Create a new ScreenGui to hold our GUI

local Label = Instance.new("TextLabel") -- Create a a new GUI Label to be in our Holder

```lua
local Location = game:GetService('Players'):GetPlayerFromCharacter(Player.Parent) -- Find Player folder for our Player

Holder.Parent = Location.PlayerGUI -- Insert the Holder into the PlayerGUI

Label.Parent = Holder -- Insert our Label into the Holder

Label.Text = "Hello " .. Player.Parent.Name -- Set the text of our Label and include the Player's name

Label.Position = UDim2.new(0, 100, 0, 100) -- Position the Label

Label.Size = UDim2.new(0, 100, 0, 100) -- Position the Label

Label.Font = "ArialBold"  -- Change the font of the Label

Label.FontSize = "Size14"  -- Change the font size of the Label

end

end
```

Button.Touched:connect(onTouch) -- Connect a
Touched event on the Part to our function

When you are sure that your Script is correct, return to the Game Window to save and exit your game.

After returning to your game in Edit Mode of ROBLOX Studio go into a Play Solo test from the File Bar:

Tools -> Test -> Play Solo

As you are testing the game, a GUI should appear on your screen after touching the Part. Tutorial successful!

Overview – GUI Appear Button

1. **GUI Text -** Text that is optional on a TextLabel, TextButton, or ImageLabel GUI.

2. **GUI Text Font -** A Font that is the appearance of the GUI Text of a GUI, which allows for text. There is a limited selection of Fonts on ROBLOX.

3. **GUI Text Size -** Size of the text on text allowing GUIs on ROBLOX.

Chapter 23

Velocity

This chapter includes a table of the different Velocity types.

This chapter will only include a short description of the different types of **Velocity** on ROBLOX. Velocity is the movement of an object on ROBLOX. Also, Velocity is a way of interaction between objects. This interaction causes one object to slide off of another in a certain direction.

A **Velocity Property** also exists in a Brick or Part. This allows for a Brick or Part to act as a conveyor belt. By this, any object that falls onto a Part with Velocity on the corresponding side will move. Some of these Objects may only be inserted by using a Free Model. These objects are:

Object	Description
BodyVelocity	Controls the speed of an object in a direction.
BodyAngularVelocity	This is a Velocity that controls angle of an object.
BodyForce	Manages the Force of an object pushing in a set direction.
BodyGyro	Causes a Brick to rotate or point in a new direction while staying in a set position.
BodyPosition	Moves a Brick to a certain location based upon a set Force/Speed.
BodyThrust	Specifies a direction for a Part to thrust towards.

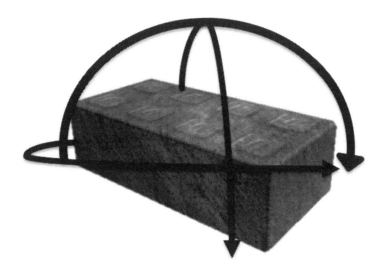

Overview – Velocity

1. **Velocity** - Movement of an object in a certain direction at a set speed.

2. **Velocity Property** - The property of a Brick to set its Velocity.

3. **BodyVelocity** - The speed of an object in a given direction.

4. **BodyAngularVelocity** - Controls the angle of an object.

5. **BodyForce** - The Force of an object pushing in a set direction.

6. **BodyGyro** - The Rotation or Pointing of a Brick or Part in a new direction while remaining in a set position.

7. **BodyPosition** - The movement of a Brick to a certain location based upon a set Speed.

8. **BodyThrust** - A direction for a Part to move towards.

Chapter 24

Tutorial 12 – Floating Platform

In this tutorial we will make a Part simulate a floating action by using BodyVelocity.

This tutorial is going to be a very short example showing the use of BodyVelocity. We will make a Part float and seem to **Hover** off of the ground. By making the Part float it will run off of a **Continuous Script** that changes the values of BodyVelocity. Since BodyVelocity works off of the gravity on its affecting object, the changing values will make the Part rise and fall.

Begin this tutorial by going into a new Empty Baseplate in Edit Mode of ROBLOX Studio. First we will add a Part from the File Bar:

Insert -> Object -> Part

To make the tutorial less bland, change the Color or this Part to Bright Red. Also, resize the Part to 4x4 studs then offset the Part from its default position and raise it up one stud. We want to offset this Brick so that we do not land on it, and we want to raise it so it is free to move. It is important to go exactly with the 4x4 studs because the BodyVelocity configurations in this tutorial work with the weight of a 4x4 Part. Select this Part in the Explorer and add a Script from the File Bar:

Insert -> Object -> Script

Next we will do a slightly different step. In order to add BodyVelocity into the Part, you have to go into the Insert Panel and search the Free Models for a BodyVelocity object. ROBLOX has removed the BodyVelocity object from directly being inserted into a Part. The steps are below:

Insert -> Object -> Inventory -> Free Models -> BodyVelocity

These are the only components that we will need. Just before we continue, set the **P Property** of BodyVelocity to 1000 to give a goal for the Brick, and cause it to be aggressive and reach its goal.

Now, double-click on the Script in the Explorer. Once the Script Editor opens clear the Script. This Script will require two **local**s. One **local** will be named *Floater* to represent our Part and the second will be named *Magic* to represent the BodyVelocity in our Part. Here are these **local**s:

local Floater = script.Parent -- Our Part

local Magic = Floater.BodyVelocity -- BodyVelocity object

Since we have **local**s to use in our Script, it is time

to declare a **function**. For this Script the **function** should be continuous, there will be no interactions needed. A continuous **function** will look like this:

while true do

After our **while true do** comes the major part of our Script. All of the following code is customized based upon the 4x4 Part we are using. We will be changing the BodyVelocity values to simulate a rise and fall in the Part's position. The following code will first have the Part rise, then wait and fall, then wait again until it will repeat endlessly:

Magic.maxForce = Vector3.new(0, 4000, 0) -- Upwards Force

Magic.velocity = Vector3.new(0, 1, 0) -- Positive Velocity

wait(2.5) -- Waits 2.5 seconds

Magic.maxForce = Vector3.new(0, 3465, 0) -- Low Force value to slow the fall of Part against gravity

Magic.velocity = Vector3.new(0, 1, 0) -- Positive Velocity

wait(.75) -- Waits .75 seconds

Lastly, the **while true do** still requires an **end** even though it repeats itself continuously:

end

Our Script is now complete; make sure that it looks like this:

local Floater = script.Parent -- Our Part

local Magic = Floater.BodyVelocity -- BodyVelocity object

while true do

Magic.maxForce = Vector3.new(0, 4000, 0) -- Upwards Force

Magic.velocity = Vector3.new(0, 1, 0) -- Positive Velocity

wait(2.5) -- Waits 2.5 seconds

Magic.maxForce = Vector3.new(0, 3465, 0) -- Low Force value to slow the fall of Part against gravity

Magic.velocity = Vector3.new(0, 1, 0) -- Positive Velocity

wait(.75) -- Waits .75 seconds

end

Before we continue, return to the Game Window to save and exit your game. Return to the game in Edit Mode of ROBLOX Studio. Conduct a test by going into a Play Solo Test in the File Bar:

Tools -> Test -> Play Solo

While in the Play Solo Test you will know that your script works if you see the platform rising and falling continuously. Return to the Game Window to save and exit. Tutorial completed!

Overview – Floating Platform

1. **Hover** - An effect that makes a Brick or Part act as if it is floating in the air without any support.

2. **Continuous Script** - A Script that repeats an infinite number of times.

3. **P Property** - The measure of aggressiveness in BodyVelocity for a Part or Brick to reach its goal.

4. **while true do** - A function in a script that repeats an infinite number of times without requiring an interaction. This starts automatically.

5. maxForce - The maximum Force exerted on any axis of a Part or Brick by BodyVelocity.

6. velocity - The speed of a Part or Brick to move by BodyVelocity.

Chapter 25

Data Persistence

In this chapter there will be an explanation of Data Persistence.

In ROBLOX a game can save in-game information of a User with **Data Persistence**. This is a system that allows the saving and loading of **Player Data**. Player Data is Player specific; a User can only load saved data that is their own. You can find this very useful for Leaderboard information in games such as **RPG**s or while saving in-game creations. Data Persistence is only functional in a ROBLOX Play Mode where ROBLOX servers are accessible.

In order to save the data of a Player the ROBLOX game has to change a value called **Data Ready** to be ready. ROBLOX has a built in function to wait for this:

game.Players.PlayerAdded:connect(**function**(Playe r)

Player:WaitForDataReady()

end)

This **function** may look different than usual, but it serves to trigger when a Player enters the game. When using a :WaitForDataReady() method, the Script does the same as a :**wait**() although lasting until the Data Ready is ready. None of this code actually loads data, it is just a preparation. After this delay you may add any needed code before loading data, such as setting up a Leaderboard value.

Data is saved in the form of a **Key**. A Key identifies different Data instances. To define a key use the following template for code:

local Key = "Value"

In order to load a Key, there are three ways. One way loads a Number, another one loads a String, and the last one loads an **Instance** of any object:

:LoadNumber(Key)

:LoadString(Key)

:LoadInstance(Key)

To load a specific Player's value, we will return to some previous code and expand. Use this code:

game.Players.PlayerAdded:connect(**function**(Playe r)

Player:WaitForDataReady()

```lua
local Score = Player:LoadNumber(Key)

    if (Key ~= nil) then

    end

end)
```

In the code above, we also make sure that **Key** has existing data to represent before using it.

   If you want to save data when a Player leaves a game, we must use a new method inside of a new **function**. There are three ways to save data, just like loading data:

```lua
:SaveNumber(Key, Score)

:SaveString(Key, Score)

:SaveInstance(Key, Score)
```

An example of one of these in action is to save a Number with this new method:

```lua
game.Players.PlayerRemoving:connect(function(Player)

local Score = Player:SaveNumber(Key, Score)
```

```
                        end)
```

We can now have these become combined into one Script, however, there will be no real data to load, so the Number will be returned as 0:

```
              local Key = "Value"

game.Players.PlayerAdded:connect(function(Playe
                          r)

           Player:WaitForDataReady()

     local Score = Player:LoadNumber(Key)

                print("" .. Score)

                        end)

game.Players.PlayerRemoving:connect(function(Pl
                        ayer)

  local Score = Player:SaveNumber(Key, Score)

                        end)
```

As a result, you now have a working Data Persistence Script which will save and load the Player Data.

Overview – Data Persistence

1. **Data Persistence -** A system that allows the saving and loading of User specific data on ROBLOX.

2. **Player Data -** Player specific data which a User can only load their own saved data.

3. **RPG -** A Role Playing Game.

4. **Data Ready -** A component in every Player in a ROBLOX Game that changes to Ready to enable Data Persistence saving and loading.

5. **:WaitForDataReady()** - Pauses the Script until the DataReady of a Player is Ready.

6. **Key -** The reference to an instance of Data in a script.

7. **Instance -** A representation of any ROBLOX game object.

Chapter 26

Tutorial 13 - Data Persistence

In this Chapter, we will combine knowledge from the previous Chapter about Data Persistence, and will create a Data Persistence Script load and save a Brick or Part color.

Data Persistence will allow a game to save the content to a specific User. In this tutorial we will save the Instance of a Part when a User has left our game. If the User re-enters the game, their saved Part will be loaded to appear above the default Part. To add more customization we will have the Part change in color when clicked. Also, we will have the Script create a Message to be displayed upon a successful load.

Go into an Empty Baseplate map in Edit Mode of ROBLOX Studio. After the game has loaded in ROBLOX Studio insert a Part from the File Bar:

Insert -> Object -> Part

This is the Part that we will be saving. First we will add two Scripts into the Part, one will act as the Data Persistence manager and the other will control the Color changing. Just do add a script twice from the File Bar:

Insert -> Object -> Script

Plus, the Color changing actions of this tutorial will require a Click Detector. Add one now into the Part from the File Bar:

Insert -> Object -> ClickDetector

Well, those are all of the components that we will need.

Continue on to one of the Scripts that we have added. It does not matter which script you choose at this point, just choose the opposite one next. Double-click on the chosen Script in the Explorer to open the Script Editor. Clear this Script, so we can make way for the Color Changing Script. You have seen this before, so this code will be very brief. First in this script will be our **local** named *Brick* for our Part:

local Brick = script.Parent -- Part

Next will come our **function**, which is a simple Click **function**:

function onClick() -- Start function

Inside of this **function** will be one line of core code. The purpose of this one line is to change the BrickColor property of **Brick** to a random Color:

Brick.BrickColor = BrickColor.Random() -- Change Brick's color to a random color

Mark an **end** to our single **function** with one **end**:

end

Lastly, to complete this script make a connection between a Click Event on our ClickDetector in **Brick** to the **function**:

Brick.ClickDetector.MouseClick:connect(onClick) -- Connect clicked event with function

The overall code of this first script should look like the following:

local Brick = script.Parent -- Part

function onClick() -- Start function

Brick.BrickColor = BrickColor.Random() -- Change Brick's color to a random color

end

Brick.ClickDetector.MouseClick:connect(onClick) -- Connect clicked event with function

Optional steps:

Return to the Game window to save and exit your game. Re-enter the game in Edit Mode of ROBLOX

Studio. Conduct a test of the current progress by going into a Play Solo test in the File Bar:

Tools -> Test -> Play Solo

When in the test, you can see if the Script is functioning properly by clicking on the Part and observing a Color change. If there is a Color change, then everything is working properly and you may return to the Game Window to continue.

Now, it is time for the second Script. In the Explorer double-click on the Script that does not contain our Color Changing **function**s to open the Script Editor. Inside of this Script will be our Data Persistence capabilities. Clear the script to begin, then add the definition of three **local**s. One **local** will be named *Brick* for our Part, another will be named *Key* for our Data Persistence Key, and the third will be named *Message* to represent a new instance of a Message. Add the following:

local Brick = script.Parent -- Part

local Key = "Part" -- A Key to hold the object we will save

local Message = Instance.new("Message") -- An

Next in this script will be methods that was taught in the previous chapter. When a Player enters the game, the following **function** will run:

game.Players.PlayerAdded:connect(**function**(Player) -- Start a function when a Player enters the game and pass them as Player

Before the **function** can continue we will use a built in command to wait for the DataReady of Player to be ready:

Player:WaitForDataReady()

This will create a pause in the Script. After the pause we will Load the Player's Instance of Key with a **local** named *Object*:

local Object = Player:LoadInstance(Key)

Even though we have loaded the Instance we need to insure that there was anything to load. We will use an **if** and **then**:

if (Object ~= **nil**) **then** -- Check to see if Object exists

Seeing if there is anything that was loaded to work with will allow us to do the following:

Object.Parent = game.Workspace -- Insert the Object

Object.Anchored = **true** -- Anchor the Object

Object.CFrame = CFrame.new(Brick.Position+Vector3.new(0, 2, 0)) -- Changes the position of Object to two studs higher than Brick

Above we have set up the saved Part represented by **Object**. We put the Part into the Workspace of our game, **Anchor** it so it will stay stationary, and move it to the same position as **Brick** but two studs higher. To show the User that this was a complete success we will display **Message**:

Message.Text = "Success" -- Set the text of the message

Message.Parent = game.Workspace -- Insert the message into the game

wait(5) -- Wait 5 seconds

Message:Remove()

In this code we make **Message** read "Success" and be displayed in the game's Workspace for 5 seconds until we then Remove it. To **end** this **function** there will two **end**s. One **end** is for **function** the and the other for the **if**. The second if will also have a closing parenthesis:

end

end)

 This Script also requires a second similar **function** for saving Data when a User leaves the game. Start the **function** as described in the previous chapter:

game.Players.PlayerRemoving:connect(**function**(Player) -- Start a function when the player leaves and pass them as Player

Only one line will be in this **function** because all we will do is save **Brick** to **Key**:

 Player:SaveInstance(Key, Brick) -- Save the Brick

Now mark an **end** with a closing parenthesis for the

function:

end)

Both of these **function**s are now complete. All together our second Script should read this code:

```
local Brick = script.Parent -- Part

local Key = "Part" -- A Key to hold the object we will save

local Message = Instance.new("Message") -- An instance of a new message

game.Players.PlayerAdded:connect(function(Player) -- Start a function when a Player enters the game and pass them as Player

Player:WaitForDataReady()

local Object = Player:LoadInstance(Key)

if (Object ~= nil) then -- Check to see if Object exists

Object.Parent = game.Workspace -- Insert the Object

Object.Anchored = true -- Anchor the Object
```

```lua
        Object.CFrame =
CFrame.new(Brick.Position+Vector3.new(0, 2, 0)) --
Changes the position of Object to two studs higher
                  than Brick

    Message.Text = "Success" -- Set the text of the
                   message

    Message.Parent = game.Workspace -- Insert the
              message into the game

         wait(5) -- Wait 5 seconds

          Message:Remove()

                  end

                end)

game.Players.PlayerRemoving:connect(function(Pl
ayer) -- Start a function when the player leaves and
              pass them as Player

Player:SaveInstance(Key, Brick) -- Save the Brick

                end)
```

Once you have verified your code, return to the
Game Window to save and exit. Since we may not

use Data Persistence in any **Game Mode** other than Play Mode, you have to Play the game to test it. Enter the game once then click on the Part to change its color. Second, leave the game and re-enter. If the Script has worked correctly you should see a Part with the same color as the color you previously changed the original Brick to. This new Part will be above the original. Finally you can exit this game. Tutorial complete!

Overview – Data Persistence

1. **Anchor -** The state of a Brick or Part that forces it to stay stationary if enabled.

2. **Game Mode -** A normal public Playing Game Mode of ROBLOX. This is the part that has multiplayer ROBLOX servers. These servers communicate directly with ROBLOX servers.

Chapter 27

InsertService

In this chapter you will learn about the ROBLOX InsertService and its uses.

In a ROBLOX game objects can be inserted from an external asset using an **InsertService** method. The InsertService method will insert a Public model that is owned by the game's creator. This method will load items from the ROBLOX website based upon their **Asset ID**. Behind this method is the functionality that allows for an advanced building game. Also, you can wait until it is absolutely necessary to take up the required **Memory** that a model will fill. Instances loaded through the InsertService are fully customizable, just as if they were a Clone.

The InsertService method can be seen in objects such as the SkateBoard. Also, ROBLOX uses the InsertService in their Insert tool or in their *Welcome to ROBLOX Building* game. InsertService will work on any type of Instance. There can be a physical object or a non-visible game component.

Here is an example on how to go about the InsertService method to load an asset:

local Object = game:GetService("InsertService"):LoadAsset(AssetI D)

```
game:GetService("InsertService"):Insert(Object)
```

Above, we use InsertService by loading the method through **GetService**. Then we use **LoadAsset** based upon the Asset ID of an item. You can find the Asset ID of an object in its website URL. The **LoadAsset** works to insert the object into our game just as a **Clone**() method would do. We can also go ahead and **Insert** it into to the game. To continue on with this method you could change the Position of the object or even the object's Name.

Overview – InsertService

1. **InsertService** - A method that allows a user to insert any object into the game that is owned by the creator of the game.

2. **Asset ID** - The corresponding ROBLOX assigned ID that goes with an object. This can be found in the website URL for the object.

3. **Memory** - The data space on a server taken up by an object. A high amount of memory usage can slow down a game's performance.

Chapter 28

Tutorial 14 - Load Model Tool

In this tutorial you will use InsertService methods to load a Model into your game when you use a tool.

In this tutorial I will demonstrate how to insert a Pre-made car model using InsertService methods. You will be working with a Tool to know when to insert the Model. Also this will be your first time using a **LocalScript**. A LocalScript is a script that works directly with Player properties.

To start, go into an Empty Baseplate in Edit Mode of ROBLOX Studio. First, we will be adding a Tool from the File Bar into the StarterPack instead of the Workspace:

Insert -> Object -> Tool

Into this tool we will need to insert a Part. Every Tool that has a Part to be held in the hands of a User requires a Part named Handle. You can change the gripped position of this Handle in the Tool's properties. Make sure you add this Part into our Tool and name it *Handle*:

Insert -> Object -> Part

Our final component will be a LocalScript. Add the LocalScript directly into the Tool from the File Bar:

Insert -> Object -> LocalScript

Double-click on the Script to open the Script Editor. Now clear the Script of its original contents before we begin adding our own code. First off will come one **local** named *Tool* for our Tool:

local Tool = script.Parent -- Tool

Secondly, we will declare the only **function** in this Script. This **function** will be connected later, and will be named to describe the interaction required to make it become triggered. Here is the code:

function onEquip() -- Find the Player based upon the script

After the **function** it is time for two more **local**, which will be of use later. One **local** is named *Player* for the Player. Second will be a **local** named *Object* for the Model to be inserted. These are the **local**s:

local Player = game.Player.LocalPlayer.Character -- Find the Player based upon the script

local Object = game:GetService("InsertService"):LoadAsset(66393 512) -- Prepare to load asset

Our Object is based off of this model:
http://www.roblox.com/Motorcycle-
item?id=66393512

With these new **local**s we are ready to add the Object into our game. To do this there will be an InsertService method and some customizations:

game:GetService("InsertService"):Insert(Object) -- Insert Object

Object.Parent = game.Workspace -- Put Object in the Workspace

Object.Name = "Car for " .. Player.Name -- Rename the Model

Finishing of the **function** is one **end**:

end

Connecting our Tool to trigger **function** once it is **Equipped**. Here is the connection:

Tool.Equipped:connect(onEquip) -- Make connection between gear being equipped and function

Check all of your code. All together it should

appear as follows:

```
local Tool = script.Parent -- Tool

function onEquip() -- Find the Player based upon
the script

local Player = game.Player.LocalPlayer.Character -
- Find the Player based upon the script

local Object =
game:GetService("InsertService"):LoadAsset(66393
512) -- Prepare to load asset

game:GetService("InsertService"):Insert(Object) --
Insert Object

Object.Parent = game.Workspace -- Put Object in
the Workspace

Object.Name = "Car for " .. Player.Name -- Rename
the Model

end

Tool.Equipped:connect(onEquip) -- Make
connection between gear being equipped and
function
```

Return to the Game Window to save and exit your game. Now, go back into the game in Edit Mode of ROBLOX Studio. Open up a Play Solo test:

Tools -> Test -> Play Solo

In the test, the Tool should insert a Car into the game once it is Equipped. Exit the Play Solo to return to the Game Window where you can save and exit. Tutorial completed!

Overview – Load Model Tool

1. **LocalScript -** A Script that works directly with Player properties.

2. **Equipped -** The term used to describe a Tool currently being used by a User.

Chapter 29

Leaderboards

This chapter will teach you about Leaderboards, the basic score system in a ROBLOX Game.

A Leaderboard is the basic in-game scoreboard. Every game can have their own values to be shown. These values could serve as the currency in a game, or as a ranking system for **Knockouts** and **Wipeouts**. Data Persistence can be used to save a Leaderboard value. Even if there is no score to be displayed, you can see the list of current Players in a Game. Also a Leaderboard can be hidden or enlarged with on-screen buttons.

Leaderboards are organized in the **Chronological Order** of the time on the server, with newest Players being on the bottom. However, your Player is always at the top as a convenience. In a sense, a Leaderboard has the same layout of a table, with columns and rows, each with their own header. Here is an example of a leaderboard in table form:

Players	Score1	Score2
Your Player	Number	Number
Player	Number	Number
Player	Number	Number
Player	Number	Number

Along with the player name is their BC status, if they have one. Plus, by clicking on the name of the Player, you can send them a Friend request. Once sent, a friend request will appear as a notification on the recipients screen for a few moments. The recipient can choose to accept, decline, or leave it pending.

Overview – Leaderboards

1. **Knockouts -** The name for the number of times once User has killed other Users. One kill would be referred to as a "Knockout".

2. **Wipeouts -** A term used to represent the number of times a User has been killed by other Users. The singular form is "Wipeout".

3. **Chronological Order -** Order based upon time, with most recent in the end and oldest at the beginning.

Chapter 30

Tutorial 15 – Creating and Manipulating a Leaderboard

This chapter will show how to create and manipulate a Leaderboard.

In this chapter you will learn first about how to create a Leaderboard. You will add a custom Value to this Leaderboard. Then, you will make the Leaderboard Value change when a Part is touched. In order to do this, you will find out how to find the Leaderboard Value based upon who touches the Part.

Enter an Empty BasePlate in Edit Mode of ROBLOX Studio. All we need are two components, a Part to serve as a trigger and a Script inside of the Part:

Insert -> Object -> Part

Then:

Insert -> Object -> Script

Good, the rest of the components will be created later in our Script. We will do this all programmatically.

Double-click on the Script to open it in the Script Editor. First, clear the Script, and declare multiple **local**s. Three **local**s will be referenced. One named *Part* for our Part, and the other two named *Leaderboard* and *Score* for two new

Instances of IntValues:

```
local Part = script.Parent -- Our Part

local Leaderboard = Instance.new("IntValue") --
New IntVaue for Leaderboard

local Score = Instance.new("IntValue") -- New
IntValue for Leaderboard section
```

Our first **function** will run when a Player enters the game, so it will pass us the new Player as Player. We will make the connection at then end of our Script, but for now just add the following:

```
function onEnter(Player) -- Function passing new
Player, as Player
```

In this **function** is the core code for creating a Leaderboard. Needed first is for Leaderboard to be named as "leaderstats", which is required. Then we will name Score as "Score" and set it to 0. Lastly, we will insert Leaderboard into Player and Score into Leaderboard:

```
Leaderboard.Name = "leaderstats" -- Name
Leaderboard, required
```

Score.Name = "Score" -- Set name to be displayed as section

Score.Name = 0 -- Set initial Score to 0

Leaderboard.Parent = Player -- Insert Leaderboard to Player

Score.Value = Leaderboard -- Insert Score into Leaderboard

Cut off the **function** with a single **end**:

end

However, this Script will also contain another **function** for changing the Score. This **function** passes us the triggering object as *Brick*:

function onTouch(Brick) -- Function passing Brick, as Trigger

Since we know how to look for a Humanoid in **Brick** as a **local**, the next few lines of code should be easy. Plus, you already know how to use an **if** and **then** to verify that a Humanoid exists in the **local**:

local Player = Brick.Parent:findFirstChild("Humanoid") -- Search for a Humanoid

if (Player ~= **nil**) **then** -- Verify that the Humanoid in Player exists

local Location = game:GetService('Players'):GetPlayerFromCharacter(Player.Parent) -- Find Player folder for our Player

Only two lines of code remain in this **function** and they use the **local** called Location. First, we will set a new **local** named *Scores* using Location to find our Score IntValue from the previous **function**. Then with the new *Scores* **local** the value of *Scores* will increase by 1:

local Part = Location.leaderstats.Score -- Find Score

Scores.Value = Scores.Value + 1 -- Increases Score by 1

Last of all for this **function**, are an **end** for the **function** and an **end** for the **if**. So two **end**s in total:

end

end

To close off the entire Script, we need to make connections between out two **function** and the events that trigger them. It does not matter where these come in the Script, I just put them in the end out of convenience:

game.Players.ChildAdded:connect(onEnter) -- Connect onEnter to new Player entering the game

Part.Touched:connect(onTouch)-- Connect a touched event to onTouch Function

This tutorial has a Script that is very long, so you may have made a small mistake. All together the Script should contain the following code:

local Part = script.Parent -- Our Part

local Leaderboard = Instance.new("IntValue") -- New IntVaue for Leaderboard

local Score = Instance.new("IntValue") -- New IntValue for Leaderboard section

function onEnter(Player) -- Function passing new Player, as Player

```lua
Leaderboard.Name = "leaderstats" -- Name
Leaderboard, required

Score.Name = "Score" -- Set name to be displayed
as section

Score.Value = 0 -- Set initial Score to 0

Leaderboard.Parent = Player -- Insert Leaderboard
to Player

Score.Parent = Leaderboard -- Insert Score into
Leaderboard

end

function onTouch(Brick) -- Function passing Brick,
as Trigger

local Player =
Brick.Parent:findFirstChild("Humanoid") -- Search
for a Humanoid

if (Player ~= nil) then -- Verify that the Humanoid in
Player exists

local Location =
game:GetService('Players'):GetPlayerFromCharact
er(Player.Parent) -- Find Player folder for our Player
```

```
local Part = Location.leaderstats.Score -- Find
Score

Scores.Value = Scores.Value + 1 -- Increases
Score by 1

end

end

game.Players.ChildAdded:connect(onEnter) --
Connect onEnter to new Player entering the game

Part.Touched:connect(onTouch)-- Connect a
touched event to onTouch Function
```

Once finished, return to the Game Window to save and exit your game. You would not want to lose all of your work now.

Finish this tutorial off by returning to the game in Edit Mode of ROBLOX Studio. Open up a Play Solo test from the File Bar:

Tools -> Test -> Play Solo

When in the Play Solo, you should observe a new Score value in the Leaderboard. If you touch the Part, the Value on the Leaderboard next to your

Name will increase by one. Pretend that the Leaderboard was a table, by default it should look like this:

Players	Score
Your Player	0

However, if it does not look like that, re-check your code again. Now return to the Game Window to once again save and exit your game. Tutorial complete!

Overview – Creating and Manipulating a Leaderboard

1. leaderstats - The required name of a Leaderboard. You can add different IntValues to this IntValue for new columns in the Leaderboard.

Chapter 31

Time of Day

This Chapter is very short because Time of Day is not a broad topic. However, it is a nice effect for any game.

I will only include this chapter to introduce the next final tutorial. This will be a very short tutorial, because the subject is only a Property. **Time of Day** on ROBLOX determines the position of the **Skybox Sun** or **Skybox Moon** in the **Skybox**. Just as in a real-life sky, the Skybox Sun and Skybox Moon move throughout the sky based upon the set Time. Also, this determines the Lighting and darkness of the Skybox.

This property can be used to make clocks, or just adjust the game lighting. Lighting can be a very good effect to change the mood of a game. Plus, this property of Lighting is accessible and editable, so it is very easy to load and change in another Script as a numerical value.

More specifically, this is the TimeOfDay property of the Lighting grouping in the Explorer. If you were to change the values of TimeOfDay they would run off of a **Military Time** basis. Military Time is a time that goes from 1 a.m to 24 p.m. So, a value of 1:00 would be the lightest and a value of 24:00 would be the darkest.

Overview – Time of Day

1. **Time of Day -** The time on a ROBLOX game which determines the lighting.

2. **Skybox Sun -** A Sky that moves around the Skybox and has its position determined by the current Time of Day.

3. **Skybox Moon -** A Moon that moves throughout the Skybox based upon the Time of Day.

4. **Skybox -** A six-sided sky and ground atmosphere around the ROBLOX Workspace.

5. TimeOfDay - This is an accessible and changeable Value that determines the Time of Day on ROBLOX.

6. **Military Time -** A standard time that goes through the full 1-24 hours instead of 1-12.

Chapter 32

Tutorial 16 – Day Changer and Clock

This chapter will include a simple Tutorial on how to first change the Time of Day in a ROBLOX game, then how to display it as a Humanoid.

In this tutorial you will be working with the Lighting to adjust Time of Day. You will make a constantly changing Time of Day Script. All results will be visual in the game **Atmosphere** and skybox. Also, you will use a Humanoid to display the TimeOfDay Property of Lighting. This Humanoid brick will **function** as a Clock. Lastly, you will be working with an IntValue.

First, go into an Empty Baseplate in Edit Mode of ROBLOX Studio. Since we are working with a Humanoid in this tutorial, we will need a Model to hold everything. This Model will also serve as the determiner of the Humanoid displaying text. Insert a Humanoid from the File Bar:

Insert -> Object -> Model

Next, add the Part that will hold our Script. Add this Part directly into the Model, and then rename the Part to *Head*. A Humanoid detects Parts named *Head* and will be displayed above the Part. Add it now from the File Bar:

Insert -> Object -> Part

Into the Part add a Script from the File Bar:

Insert -> Object -> Script

One of the most important components is next, add a Humanoid into the Model from the File Bar:

Insert -> Object -> Humanoid

Make sure that you set the MaxHealth Property of the Humanoid to 0 so that no Health Bar is displayed along with the Humanoid Text. Last of all, add an IntValue which will help later to keep track of the Hour we will set the Time of Day as. This is also in the File Bar, and will be added into our Part:

Insert -> Object -> Model

It is time to make our Script, double-click on the Script to open the Script Editor. After you clear the Script, declare our **local**s. A **local** will be needed for our Model and IntValue, name these *Model* and *Time*:

local Model = script.Parent.Parent -- Our Model

local Time = script.Parent.Value -- Our IntValue

After the **local**s there must be a continuous type of **function** declared:

while true do

Inside of the **function** lies code that will always repeat with the **while true do**. First, since TimeOfDay in Lighting is based on Military time, the max value we ever want Time to be is 24. There will be an **if** which can check if Time is equal to 24. If it is Time must be reset to 0. Make this entire **if** and **then** come first in the **while true do**:

if Time.Value == 24 **then** -- Check if Time value is 24

Time.Value = 0 -- Set Time value to 0

end

On the other hand, if Time is not equal to 24 the Script can continue. In order for Time to change, we will increase it by 1 every time the **while true do** runs:

Time.Value = Time.Value + 1 -- Add one to Time value

With this newly determined Time, the Script will do three things. One, it will change the Lighting's TimeOfDay to Time. Second, it will change Model's

Name to **Time** so that the Humanoid will work as a Clock. Third and last, our Script will wait 1 second until it repeats:

game.Lighting.TimeOfDay = Time.Value -- Set TimeOfDay to Time value

Model.Name = Time.Value .. ":00" -- Set text for Humanoid

wait(1) -- Wait 1 second

Lastly, **end** the **while true do**:

end

    This is a relatively short Script, so it will be very easy to check. Compare your code to this:

local Model = script.Parent.Parent -- Our Model

local Time = script.Parent.Value -- Our IntValue

while true do

if Time.Value == 24 **then** -- Check if Time value is 24

Time.Value = 0 -- Set Time value to 0

end

Time.Value = Time.Value + 1 -- Add one to Time value

game.Lighting.TimeOfDay = Time.Value -- Set TimeOfDay to Time value

Model.Name = Time.Value .. ":00" -- Set text for Humanoid

wait(1) -- Wait 1 second

end

Return to the Game Window to save and exit your game.

Go back into the game in Edit Mode of ROBLOX Studio. Continue into a Play Solo test from the File Bar:

Tools -> Test -> Play Solo

In the Play Solo you should see the effects visually as the Lighting changes. Also the Skybox Sun and Skybox Moon will move across the Skybox. Plus, the Humanoid Part will display a constantly changing time. Once again, return to the Game

Window to save and exit your game. Tutorial
Completed.

Overview – Day Changer and Clock

---

1. **Atmosphere -** The surrounding environment of a ROBLOX game. This includes dynamic effects such as the Lighting.

Chapter 33

ROBLOX History

Want to know more about ROBLOX? Here is a short summary of the ROBLOX History as a company.

ROBLOX was first introduced in 2004 by its two founders **David Baszucki** and **Erik Cassel**. David Baszucki is the current CEO of ROBLOX. You can find him on his ROBLOX account, which is david.baszucki. Erick Cassel is the Chief Scientist. His ROBLOX username is Erik.Cassel.

The first user on ROBLOX was created in June of 2004. His username is Admin. At one point the **User ID** of Admin changed from *1* to *18*. In September of 2004 ROBLOX went into **Alpha**. Alpha is a very early testing stage. This early Alpha stage ended in early 2005. The major ROBLOX administrative user named *ROBLOX* was also created in 2005. ROBLOX is the default user for hosting items in the catalog and official ROBLOX games. Although ROBLOX is an administrative account, the complete ROBLOX staff shares it.

ROBLOX's second year 2006 was a big year. The company gained one of their most popular employees to date named John Shedletsky. He is currently the Creative Director at ROBLOX. John Shedletsky's username on ROBLOX is Shedletsky, and he hosts the popular game known as *Sword Fights on the Heights IV*. Also in 2006 was the creation of ROBLOX's signature game known as the Crossroads. Later in the year was the start of the **ROBLOX Developer Blog**. Most importantly in this year (sorry John Shedletsky), was when ROBLOX hit the 10,000-user landmark. Lastly, the **User Profile Badges** originated. These badges include the **Bloxxer Badge**.

In 2007 ROBLOX released **User Animations**. User animations make ROBLOX characters have the appearance of movement with their limbs. Also released about the Character was **Body Colors** and T-Shirts. These Body Colors allow for different Parts of a Character to be different customizable Colors. ROBLOX's original *Happy Home in Robloxia* was created during this year; this game is now a standard for any game to be reverted to. Early in 2007 was also the ROBLOX **Report Abuse** button. The ROBLOX Wiki was created in 2007, this is the go to for all ROBLOX instructions. Some more 2007 features were Tools, Teams, Copylocking games, Supersafe chat, User-sold T-Shirts, Force-fields, Tickets, Commenting, and **Builders Club**. Lastly, ROBLOX hit 50,000 users in 2007.

2008 was the year that I joined ROBLOX. Many new features were releases such as Shirts, Pants, Decals, Heads, Walkspeed, Team Chat, and User Advertisements. Another big feat in 2008 was the ability to play as an unregistered Guest.

Next was 2009, which held the release of many new building components. One building component was the **Truss**. Plus, new materials started to arrive such as Wood and Ice. One of the biggest releases in the later years of ROBLOX was a BC upgrade including **TBC** and **OBC**, which would forever start to segregate the Users. Also, ROBLOX released **Groups**. More new in-game components were the highly anticipated GUIs, Smoke, and Bubble Chat. Lastly, the Catalog came out with Limited items and the website released an **Instant Chat** feature between friends.

2010 brings another big ROBLOX year with the creation of **ROBLOX Game Cards**. A big Character appearance change was introduced with **Body Packages**, and the **Triple Hat Glitch**. Contests are brought into the spotlight for builders and voters to receive prizes. Yet more segregation between BC and regular users came in 2010 with

BC Only Games. Lastly, Sets came out in 2010 to bring together an easier grouping of Models.

2011 is one of the biggest years in ROBLOX history. So many new content and client additions became a reality. As a plus for BC Users, ROBLOX released the BC Loyalty program that offers additional **Robux** for long-term BC subscribers. Groups gained the ability to advertise, declare allies/enemies, or become Primary to a User. Games can now be recorded with an in-game **Video Recorder** and **Screenshot** capturer. My ROBLOX iOS and Mac applications along with ROBLOX's were released onto the Apple App Store. Data Persistence comes out along with Mega Places and **Personal Servers**. ROBLOX hosts its first major ROBLOX Rally.

This year, which is 2012, is still in the very beginning and the 2012 ROBLOX Game conference has been announced. Lastly, a ROBLOX Mac client is released.

Much of the information provided by this chapter is courtesy of a ROBLOX User-run Wiki.

ROBLOX User Wiki -

Overview – ROBLOX History

1. **David Baszucki -** One of the two founders of ROBLOX. The Current CEO of ROBLOX. His username is david.baszucki

2. **Erik Cassel -** Second Founder of ROBLOX. The Chief Scientist. His ROBLOX username is Erik.Cassel.

3. **User ID -** The number of a User of ROBLOX. This can be found in the URL of a User's Profile. (Ex. ID: 1 was the first user to register)

4. **Alpha -** An early stage of testing.

5. **ROBLOX Developer Blog -** Official ROBLOX Blog for ROBLOX announces.

6. **User Profile Badges -** Badges found on the Profile of a User to signify achievements.

7. **Bloxxer Badge -** A badge won by obtaining 250 kills against other players, and less deaths than kills.

8. **User Animations -** Animations to show motion on a Character, such as arm and leg movement.

9. **Body Colors -** The option to choose different customizable colors for different body parts of a User's Character.

10. **Report Abuse -** A button that allows any User to report the actions of another User.

11. **Builders Club -** The initial paid upgrade purchasable in subscription amounts that grants bonus features to a User.

12. **Truss -** A special Brick type that has the appearance of a building beam structure.

13. **TBC -** Turbo Builders Club is the second paid upgrade purchasable in different subscription amounts that grants even more bonus features to a User than standard Builders Club.

14. **OBC -** Outrageous Builders Club is the premium paid upgrade purchasable in different subscription amounts that grants even more bonus features to a User than standard Builders Club and Turbo Builders Club.

15. **Groups -** A purchasable feature where a User can bring together other Users for a certain cause.

16. **Instant Chat -** The website chat feature that allows for quick communication between multiple Users.

17. **ROBLOX Game Cards -** Cards purchasable at retail locations that can be redeemed for certain online purchases.

18. **Body Packages -** Purchasable Body types to change the shape and appearance of a

Character's body part(s).

19. **Triple Hat Glitch -** The now accepted feature that allows a User to wear up to three hats at a time.

20. **BC Only Games -** Games that are only playable by a User with any type of Builders Club.

21. **Robux -** The premium currency that is only given out through an online purchase or to Builders Club subscribers.

22. **Video Recorder -** An in-game feature, which records the screen of a User for a gameplay video.

23. **Screenshot -** An in-game feature that takes a snapshot of a User's screen.

24. **Personal Servers -** Servers hosted by a Player instead of a typical ROBLOX game. These servers are automatically saved in certain time increments for building with large amounts of Users.

Chapter 34

About Me

In this chapter you will find out about the author, Brandon LaRouche.

Hello, my name is Brandon LaRouche, and I was born in June of 1996. When I was born, my family lived in Stockton California. I am an identical mirror twin. This means that I look the same as my brother except he is a left-handed while I am a right-handed. The name of my brother is Ryan LaRouche. Also I have a sister named Brianna who was born in 1993. My parents are John and Brenda LaRouche.

Currently I live in the town of North Attleboro, which is located in the state of Massachusetts. In my household are my brother, my parents, and myself. At this time, my sister is off in college. All throughout my childhood my Dad has been an IT Director at the same company. When I was in elementary school my Mom became a Math teacher.

I first joined ROBLOX in 2008. A year later in 2009 I began serious coding starting with HTML. In prior years I had always been interested in engineering kits and science "toys". After receiving an iPod Touch as a Christmas present in 2009 I was looking for a way to make my own ideas come to life. As a technology loving and inspirational

Dad, he started to help me find a way to develop for iOS devices. In my possession was a Dell laptop, and at the time it was impossible to develop any sort of iOS app on a Windows computer. Seeing this dilemma, my parents decided to help me and make sure that I was serious about iOS development. By deciding to help me, they split the cost of a used Macbook Pro on Ebay.

I find it very important as I look back on a few years ago in 2010 when I see how I payed for half of my Mac. This was a smart way for my parents to ensure that I was serious and that I would take great care of the computer. Once receiving my Macbook I immediately went to the book store with my Dad and we spent hours finding the right book. I eventually decided to buy a full-color iOS Programming Tutorial book (the name is not mentioned in this book). Excited as I was, I took the time to go through the book so I could have the basic knowledge for my first iOS application. At first my Dad had been learning with me, but he had a busy life with work and I soon surpassed his knowledge. My first idea for an app came to me when I was helping my Dad with a chore and came across a plastic Drill Gauge. A Drill Gauge allows screws and bolts to be compared based on the metric or US diameter. Since I was just beginning with my programming skills, the app has simple functionality and a straight-forward concept.

Within a few weeks of developing my first application on a Free Apple Developer account I was finally ready to upgrade to a full license. My parents also split this cost with me. While registering for a license I had to use my Dad's name, John LaRouche, to fulfill and 18 or older requirement. My family helped me come up with the name for my company and we finally thought of "Double Trouble Studio" to symbolize how I am a twin. Also the name represent t-shirts that my brother and I used to as little kids that said "Double Trouble". Weeks passed as my enrollment to the Developer Program was pending. When I finally received my license, I submitted my first application and had it rejected after a week of waiting. After making some minimal changes and resubmitting my application it was finally accepted. As a beginning developer, my application did not receive many downloads and stayed at a steady low 20 or below daily downloads with a Free price tag.

After releasing three more iOS applications, I first contacted ROBLOX in the summer of 2010 with a working mockup of the idea that eventually came to look like the My ROBLOX and somewhat like the ROBLOX Mobile applications. After multiple tries of talking on the Forums and to ROBLOX support the CEO of ROBLOX, David Baszucki, finally contacted me with interests in my mock-up. For ROBLOX security reasons, and after being forwarded to a technology team, I was unable to receive help with gathering user credentials for my application data. With a determined mind, I set out to create a different ROBLOX application and within a short amount of time i had the first versions of my The ROBLOX Wiki and Level Calculator for ROBLOX apps. I heard no response from ROBLOX on these so I waited 6 months from the Fall of 2010 to the Spring of 2011 when I finally went ahead and submitted my two applications.

These two applications got me the attention that was needed and I got appropriate legal permission. I was on my way to work on the 9 total iOS applications I have to this point. My most achieved application is the My ROBLOX application, which has seen my ROBLOX application dreams come true with my own personal technology innovations for the core functionality. After some time I also submitted my first iPad applications and other iPhone/iPod Touch applications that were not solely related to ROBLOX. In the end of 2011, I finally started Mac application development and now have two Mac applications, including one that is ROBLOX related.

When I am writing this book I have over 18 total applications. I have learned a lot from the development and since I have started iOS programming. If you ever have an idea or dream, just go for it. Ask your parents to help you, there is never a bad time to start! Follow your dreams, because if you do not try you will never succeed.

My Current ROBLOX iOS and Mac Applications

1. The ROBLOX Wiki (iOS)

2. Level Calculator for ROBLOX (iOS)

3. Mobile ROBLOX News (iOS)

4. The ROBLOX Quiz (iOS)

5. My ROBLOX (iOS)

6. Tutorial for ROBLOX (iOS)

7. The ROBLOX Browser (Mac)

8. ROBLOX Browser (iPad)

9. Mobile ROBLOX Developer Blog (iOS)

10. The ROBLOX Idea Generator (iOS)

All of the applications are published either on the Mac Store or Apple App Store. I have published these under my company's name - Double Trouble Studio.

Chapter 35

Tutorial Sources

Links to public version of every Tutorial.

All code can be found on the ROBLOX User BookTutorial. These games are all open source to provide fully working code for every tutorial.

BookTutorial -
http://www.roblox.com/User.aspx?ID=23665151

Source Code Links

---

1. **Tutorial 1 - No Link**

2. **Tutorial 2 - http://www.roblox.com/Tutorial-2-place?id=71625725**

3. **Tutorial 3 - http://www.roblox.com/Tutorial-3-place?id=73894935**

4. **Tutorial 4 - http://www.roblox.com/Tutorial-4-place?id=73895097**

5. **Tutorial 5 - http://www.roblox.com/Tutorial-5-place?id=73895561**

6. **Tutorial 6 - http://www.roblox.com/Tutorial-6-place?id=73895730**

7. **Tutorial 7 - http://www.roblox.com/Tutorial-7-place?id=73895765**

8. **Tutorial 8 - http://www.roblox.com/Tutorial-8-place?id=73895836**

9. Tutorial 9 - http://www.roblox.com/Tutorial-9-place?id=73895866

10. Tutorial 10 - http://www.roblox.com/Tutorial-10-place?id=73895911

11. Tutorial 11 - http://www.roblox.com/Tutorial-11-place?id=73895966

12. Tutorial 12 - http://www.roblox.com/Tutorial-12-place?id=73895985

13. Tutorial 13 - http://www.roblox.com/Tutorial-13-place?id=73896031

14. Tutorial 14 - http://www.roblox.com/Tutorial-14-place?id=73896060

15. Tutorial 15 - http://www.roblox.com/Tutorial-15-place?id=73896117

All you need to do is visit these games in Edit Mode of ROBLOX Studio to view the components. Plus, you can copy and paste any object.

Chapter 36

Combined Overview

A complete glossary of every overview term found in this book.

Overview – Basics of ROBLOX Lua

6. **Script** - A special text-file that contains a portion of a game's overall code.

7. **Scripting** - The act of programming a script in ROBLOX Lua.

8. **Workspace** - Serves as an organizing container/folder for all of your game components.

9. **Brick** - The basic component of a ROBLOX game, it is a virtual brick that you build with.

10. **Lighting** - A folder that contains every object that does not need to be seen in the actual ROBLOX game.

11. **Explorer Panel** - A side panel showing all of the folders and groups of a game's content.

12. **Players (*Folder*)** - A folder, which contains all of the player's individual content in a game.

13. **PlayerGUI** - A folder containing users' active GUI(s).

14. **GUI** - Stands for *graphical user interface*; an object in an overlaying 2D layer on the user's screen (ex. leaderboard).

15. **StarterGui** - Where all user-created GUI(s) are

placed into in order for it to be added to a player's PlayerGui when they enter a game.

16. **StarterPack -** Where any gear is placed that a player will receive when they spawn or respawn.

17. **Debris -** A folder in the Explorer Panel which is not discussed much in this book.

18. **SoundService -** A folder in the Explorer Panel which is not discussed much in this book.

19. **Property -** A manipulatable feature or quality of any object in a ROBLOX Game.

20. **Property Panel -** A panel displaying all properties of an object that can be changed.

21. **ROBLOX Studio -** ROBLOX's downloadable client that enables Edit Mode for advanced building in games. This is separate from the ROBLOX game client.

22. **Edit Mode -** A mode in ROBLOX Studio that offers a more advanced building environment than the normal Build Mode. Included are many panels and an increased number of features options such as redo/undo, rotate, pause-play-stop, etc. Programming is made easier in Edit Mode, which allows for the game's physics to be paused so other scripts or a objects do not ruin your game.

23. **Build Mode -** ROBLOX's classical building environment in which the game's physics are

constantly running and user's avatar is present to use in-game building tools.

Overview – Setting Up A Game

24. **Places -** A page of a user's account on ROBLOX showing a list of all of their games.

25. **Game's Page -** The webpage dedicated to an individual game on ROBLOX.

26. **Options -** A drop-down button which is located to the right of your a user's picture on one of their Game's Page.

27. **Configure This Place -** A button in the Options drop-down button.

28. **Configure Place Page -** Where a user can manipulate their game's settings.

29. **Description -** Description of a game seen by any user.

30. **VIP Shirt -** Clothing sold to a user for extra features in a game, most commonly sold as a t-shirt.

31. **Name -** Title or Name of a game seen by any user.

32. **Games Page -** One of the main pages on

ROBLOX.com where you can see a list of user games.

33. **Place Type -** Where a game can be set up as a Game Place or as a Personal Server.

34. **Game Place -** A game that only the user who created the game can edit, but anyone can enter.

35. **Personal Server -** A mode that any player can build in and have their changes automatically saved.

36. **Player Limit -** The amount of players allowed into your game at one time on an individual Server.

37. **Server -** An individual instance of any game, an additional server is created whenever the Player Limit has been reached.

38. **Classic Place -** A game with a max Player Limit of 20 players on one server.

39. **Mega Place -** A game with a set Player Limit of 30 (may increase in a later update).

40. **Access/Privileges -** The privacy level of a game.

41. **Public -** A game that anyone can play.

42. **Friends Only -** A game where only players on the game creator's friends list can play.

43. **Copy Protection -** Controls access levels to a

game's content towards other users.

44. **Copy-Lock -** If enabled, it locks a game so that no other user besides the game's creator can access the build or edit mode.

45. **Turn Comments On/Off -** Options that control if a game allows user commenting.

46. **Chat Settings -** Manage the the in-game chat appearance by three choices.

47. **Classic Chat -** A chat that appears as an overlaying GUI in the upper left corner of the game window on a user's screen

48. **Bubble Chat -** If enabled it creates a bubble with the user's typed message over their head when they chat.

49. **Both Chats -** Grants the ability to use both Classic Chat and Bubble Chat in a game.

50. **Genre -** A chosen category that matches a game's theme and is used in order for ROBLOX to be able to organize games.

51. **Gear Settings -** Options to allow All Genres of gear to be used in a game, Only Genres that match a game's genre, or Specific types of gear.

52. **Reset Place -** Where a game can be reverted to a preset map.

53. **Version History -** Where the game's creator

can see a list of all previous times they have saved their game. This is also where a game can be reverted back to a previous save.

54. **Overview -** Section at the end of each Chapter of this book that defines key words.

Overview – ROBLOX Studio Elements

55. **Game Engine -** A program that assists in building games. They handle physics, compiling code, interface layout, and ease up on the workload and experience required to create games.

56. **Scripting Tools -** Tools that help you with your scripting in ROBLOX Studio.

57. **View (*Pull Down*) -** Contains the option to show or hide many helpful scripting tools.

58. **File Bar -** The top bar with different tabs such as *File* or *View*.

59. **Toolbox -** A panel, which serves as a Catalog for any ROBLOX item that can be added into a ROBLOX game.

60. **Catalog -** A collection of items. On ROBLOX it is a collection of all assets created by users and staff.

61. **Free Models** - Models shared by other users in the public domain that is free for anyone to use.

62. **My Models** - Models that can be found in a user's inventory.

63. **Decals** - Images uploaded to ROBLOX and approved by the moderators.

64. **Packages** - Groupings of Free Models made by a user.

65. **Output** - An activity console that shows you the events that ROBLOX Studio has processed successfully or unsuccessfully.

66. **Diagnostic** - A panel that shows the performance of your running ROBLOX game.

67. **Task Scheduler** - A view that displays all of the current tasks being performed by ROBLOX Studio such as mesh rendering.

Overview – Hello World

68. **Script Editor** - A new window in ROBLOX Studio that acts as a color-coded text editor for ROBLOX scripts.

69. **local** - A definition that allows access to objects with a common name instead of a long reference string of code.

70. **Comment** - Text comments that mark your

code but do not change the functionality of a script. A comment is marked by "--".

71. **Parent -** Term that means that an is Parented by another object (ex. Workspace is parented by the Game).

72. **Game Window -** A window in ROBLOX Studio that allows you to view and edit your game, visible in Edit Mode.

73. **Play Solo -** A test mode with a private server and only one character; A private environment of your game.

74. **Test Player -** A player in Edit Mode's Play Solo named "Player".

Overview – Brick Properties

75. **Appearance -** Visual characteristic viewable in Edit Mode.
76. **Data -** Physical and unseen traits of a Brick or Part.

77. **Behavior -** Grouping that has to do with the way users can interact with a Brick or Part.

78. **Part (*Grouping*) -** Category controlling a Brick's or Part's interaction with the environment.

79. **Stud -** One unit of measurement for an object in a ROBLOX game.

80. **Surface Inputs** - *Not covered in this chapter.*

81. **Surface** - This grouping is the control over the Surface Connection of a Brick or Part.

82. **Surface Connection** - The type and strength of the hold between the sides of two objects.

Overview – Color Changing Door

83. **Door** - A Brick or Part that opens and closes to allow a player to enter an area.

84. **Part** - Also known as a Brick. The basic component of a ROBLOX game, it is a virtual object that you build with.

85. **function** - An action that restrict the script to only trigger when a certain action takes place.

86. **end** - A call that closes a **function**.

87. **CanCollide** - Property of a brick that determines if a brick is solid or not.

88. **true/false** - Two choices of certain properties that enable or disable the property.

89. **Transparency** - The level of translucence of an object.

90. **Color** - The color of an object.

91. **BrickColor** - The color of a Brick or Part that is based off of a number system.

92. **Random** - An unpredictably generated property.

93. **Touched** - Registers that an object was touched by a humanoid.

Overview – VIP Door

94. **VIP Door** - Door that only opens for a user wearing a corresponding item of clothing.

95. **VIP Shirt** - Shirt that grants special abilities in a game.

96. **:findFirstChild**("") - Searches for a designated item's Classname in the identified object or grouping.

97. **Humanoid** - A special component that can be added to an object to give it life properties in ROBLOX such as health. Any Player contains a Humanoid.

98. **if** - Used to compare values in scripts to determine whether or not to continue with an action. Every **if** needs an **end**, to signify its completion.

99. **then** - Works after an **if** to pass on the actions, only if the **if** was successful.

100. **Texture** - Image reference in ROBLOX. Used on Decals, Meshes, and clothing.

101. **Giver** - When touched by a user it automatically adds a Tool.

102. **Tool** - A ROBLOX in-game item used by a user to interact with the environment.

Overview – Player Assets and Properties

103. **StarterGear** - Holds everything from the StarterPack that contains the gear a Player will respawn with.

104. **Backpack** - Contains all of the gear that a Player has at the current moment in their inventory.

105. **Sound** - A noise that is played when an action occurs on ROBLOX.

Overview – Lava

106. **Lava** - A Brick or Part that kills or damages a user who touches it.

107. **Spawn** - An object that a user comes back to life on or starts the game on in ROBLOX. The act of coming back to life on ROBLOX.

108. Slate - A type of Material for a Brick or Part.

109. MaxHealth - The maximum or full health value for a Humanoid.

Overview – Special Effect Components

---

110. Sparkles - Star shaped objects flying outwards from a brick.

111. Forcefield - A special barrier around an object.

112. Smoke - A smog-like overlaying smoke that blocks the view of distant objects.

113. Flames - Smoke-like fire that flows in an upward velocity by default.

114. Material - Texture and appearance of a Brick or Part, that also influences traits determining interactions with the environment (ex. Stone, wood).

115. BilboardGUI - A GUI that appears over a Brick or Part and rotates to increase/decrease in size as a user comes into range.

Overview – Hat Changer

116. Hat - Object worn on the Head of a Player.

117. Programmatic Table - A non-visual table created solely for the use of a script.

118. Column - Vertical segment of a table.

119. Row - Horizontal segment of a table.

120. for - A call that passes the proceeding code based upon a series of objects.

121. do - Passes the content of a **for** call.

Overview – Basics of CFrame

122. CFrame - Stands for Coordinate Frame and represents the positioning and rotation of a Part or Brick.

123. Matrix - A mathematical array of geometric and 3D coordinates.

124. Constructor - A new instance of a CFrame position.

125. Vector3 - Movement of an object by sliding.

Overview – Teleporter

126. **Teleporter -** A Part that moves a user from one location to another instantaneously.

127. **Trigger -** Object that sends an action.

128. **Receiver -** Object that receives an action.

129. **Group -** Multiple Parts contained in the same Model, under one Parent.

130. **Model -** A grouping of Parts that are brought together by the same Parent.

Overview – Working With Strings

131. **String -** A basic text value used to define any property with text.

132. **Integer -** A number value. (ex. 100)

Overview – Random Number Humanoid

133. **Math -** Mathematical interactions between integers - numerical values.

134. **ClickDetector -** Detects a click on a Brick or

Part to trigger a **function**.

135. **math** - A call that marks the beginning of a mathematical function.

136. **random**() - Subclass of a math call to generate a random number between a certain range.

Overview – Script Functions and Methods

---

137. **Function** - Built in calls to a script.
138. **Method** - Useful services beginning with a : and ending with an ().

Overview – Click Clone

---

139. **MouseClick** - An event when a ClickDetector is clicked by a User to trigger a **function**.

140. **Value** - A numerical property of certain objects.

Overview – Starterback, Backpack, and Tools

---

141. **Tools** - An item, which a User uses to interact with the environment.

142. StarterPack - Location for all permanent Tools in a game to be placed, which any User will always receive when they spawn.

143. BackPack - A grouping, which holds the current Tools of a User.

Overview – Giver

---

144. Game:GetService('Players'):GetPlayerFromCh **aracter**() - A service which finds the corresponding Player Folder from a Character.

Overview – ROBLOX User GUIs

---

145. Visible Property - If enabled, a GUI will become visible on the screen of a User.

Overview – GUI Appear Button

---

146. GUI Text - Text that is optional on a TextLabel, TextButton, or ImageLabel GUI.

147. GUI Text Font - A Font that is the appearance of the GUI Text of a GUI, which allows for text. There is a limited selection of Fonts on ROBLOX.

148. GUI Text Size - Size of the text on text allowing GUIs on ROBLOX.

Overview – Velocity

149. Velocity - Movement of an object in a certain direction at a set speed.

150. Velocity Property - The property of a Brick to set its Velocity.

151. BodyVelocity - The speed of an object in a given direction.

152. BodyAngularVelocity – Controls the angle of an object.

153. BodyForce - The Force of an object pushing in a set direction.

154. BodyGyro - The Rotation or Pointing of a Brick or Part in a new direction while remaining in a set position.

155. BodyPosition - The movement of a Brick to a certain location based upon a set Speed.

156. BodyThrust - A direction for a Part to move towards.

Overview – Floating Platform

157. Hover - An effect that makes a Brick or Part act as if it is floating in the air without any support.

158. Continuous Script - A Script that repeats an infinite number of times.

159. P Property - The measure of aggressiveness in BodyVelocity for a Part or Brick to reach its goal.

160. while true do - A function in a script that repeats an infinite number of times without requiring an interaction. This starts automatically.

161. maxForce - The maximum Force exerted on any axis of a Part or Brick by BodyVelocity.

162. velocity - The speed of a Part or Brick to move by BodyVelocity.

Overview – Data Persistence

---

163. Data Persistence - A system that allows the saving and loading of User specific data on ROBLOX.

164. Player Data - Player specific data which a User can only load their own saved data.

165. RPG - A Role Playing Game.

166. Data Ready - A component in every Player in a ROBLOX Game that changes to Ready to enable Data Persistence saving and loading.

167. :WaitForDataReady() - Pauses the Script until

the DataReady of a Player is Ready.

168. **Key** - The reference to an instance of Data in a script.

169. **Instance** - A representation of any ROBLOX game object.

Overview – Data Persistence

---

170. **Anchor** - The state of a Brick or Part that forces it to stay stationary if enabled.

171. **Game Mode** - A normal public Playing Game Mode of ROBLOX. This is the part that has multiplayer ROBLOX servers. These servers communicate directly with ROBLOX servers.

Overview – InsertService

---

172. **InsertService** - A method that allows a user to insert any object into the game that is owned by the creator of the game.

173. **Asset ID** - The corresponding ROBLOX assigned ID that goes with an object. This can be found in the website URL for the object.

174. **Memory** - The data space on a server taken up by an object. A high amount of memory usage can slow down a game's performance.

Overview – Load Model Tool

175. LocalScript - A script that works directly with Player properties.

176. Equipped - The term used to describe a Tool currently being used by a User.

Overview – Leaderboards

177. Knockouts - The name for the number of times once User has killed other Users. One kill would be referred to as a "Knockout".

178. WipeOuts - A term used to represent the number of times a User has been killed by other Users. The singular form is "Wipeout".

179. Chronological Order - Order based upon time, with most recent in the end and oldest at the beginning.

Overview – Creating and Manipulating a Leaderboard

180. leaderstats - The required name of a Leaderboard to have. You can add different IntValues to this IntValue for new columns in the Leaderboard.

Overview – Time of Day

181. Time of Day - The time on a ROBLOX game which determines the lighting.

182. Skybox Sun - A Sky that moves around the Skybox and has its position determined by the current Time of Day.

183. Skybox Moon - A Moon that moves throughout the Skybox based upon the Time of Day.

184. Skybox - A six-sided sky and ground atmosphere around the ROBLOX Workspace.

185. TimeOfDay - This is an accessible and editable Value that determines the Time of Day on ROBLOX.

186. Military Time - A standard time that goes through the full 1-24 hours instead of 1-12.

Overview – Day Changer and Clock

187. Atmosphere - The surrounding environment of a ROBLOX game. This includes dynamic effects such as the Lighting.

Overview – ROBLOX History

188. David Baszucki - One of the two founders of ROBLOX. The Current CEO of ROBLOX. His username is david.baszucki

189. Erik Cassel - Second Founder of ROBLOX. The Chief Scientist. His ROBLOX username is Erik.Cassel.

190. User ID - The number of a User of ROBLOX. This can be found in the URL of a User's Profile. (Ex. ID: 1 was the first user to register)

191. Alpha - An early stage of testing.

192. ROBLOX Developer Blog - Official ROBLOX Blog for ROBLOX announces.

193. User Profile Badges - Badges found on the Profile of a User to signify achievements.

194. Bloxxer Badge - A badge won by obtaining 250 kills against other players, and less deaths than kills.

195. User Animations - Animations to show motion on a Character, such as arm and leg movement.

196. Body Colors - The option to choose different customizable colors for different body parts of a User's Character.

197. Report Abuse - A button that allows any User

to report the actions of another User.

198. Builders Club - The initial paid upgrade purchasable in subscription amounts that grants bonus features to a User.

199. Truss - A special Brick type that has the appearance of a building beam structure.

200. TBC - Turbo Builders Club is the second paid upgrade purchasable in different subscription amounts that grants even more bonus features to a User than standard Builders Club.

201. OBC - Outrageous Builders Club is the premium paid upgrade purchasable in different subscription amounts that grants even more bonus features to a User than standard Builders Club and Turbo Builders Club.

202. Groups - A purchasable feature where a User can bring together other Users for a certain cause.

203. Instant Chat - The website chat feature that allows for quick communication between multiple Users.

204. ROBLOX Game Cards - Cards purchasable at retail locations that can be redeemed for certain online purchases.

205. Body Packages - Purchasable Body types to change the shape and appearance of a Character's body part(s).

206. Triple Hat Glitch - The now accepted feature that allows a User to wear up to three hats at a time.

207. BC Only Games - Games that are only playable by a User with any type of Builders Club.

208.Robux - The premium currency that is only given out through an online purchase or to Builders Club subscribers.

209. Video Recorder - An in-game feature, which records the screen of a User for a gameplay video.

210. Screenshot - An in-game feature that takes a snapshot of a User's screen.

211. Personal Servers - Servers hosted by a Player instead of a typical ROBLOX game. These servers are automatically saved in certain time increments for building with large amounts of Users.

Chapter 37

Sources

Sources that have helped me when I was writing this book.

Sources

1. ROBLOX - http://www.roblox.com

2. ROBLOX Wiki - http://www.wiki.roblox.com

3. ROBLOX User Wiki - http://roblox.wikia.com/wiki/History_of_ROBLOX

Chapter 39

Contact Me

Do you have any feedback? I want to know!

Do you have any feedback? Suggestions, comments, new ideas, or issues? I value every opinion! Let me know what you think about this book! If you have any ideas or suggestions, please contact me:

Website: http://doubletroublestudio.com

Email: cowbear@verizon.net

Address: 130 John Rezza Drive North Attleboro, Massachusetts - 02763

ROBLOX Username: cowbear16

Any type of suggestions will do, I will take everything into consideration.

Thanks for Reading!